Keyboard Player's
Chord Bible

Keyboard Player's
Chord Bible

Paul Lennon

CHARTWELL
BOOKS, INC.

A QUARTO BOOK

Published in 2008 by
Chartwell Books
A division of Book Sales, Inc.
114 Northfield Avenue
Edison, New Jersey 08837
USA

ISBN13: 978-0-7858-2455-8
ISBN10: 0-7858-2455-3
QUAR.KPCB

This book was designed and produced by
Quarto Publishing plc
The Old Brewery
6 Blundell Street
London N7 9BH

Project Editor: Chloe Todd Fordham
Managing Art Editor: Anna Plucinska
Designer: Jon Wainwright
Photographer: Paul Forrester
Proofreader: Ruth Patrick
Indexer: Diana LeCore

Art Director: Caroline Guest
Creative Director: Moira Clinch
Publisher: Paul Carslake

Manufactured by Modern Age Repro House Ltd,
Hong Kong
Printed by Midas Printing International
Limited, China

10 9 8 7 6 5 4 3 2 1

Contents

Chord directory

* For quick reference to the symbols used in this book, see the fold-out flap opposite page 253

Foreword

Welcome to the *Keyboard Player's Chord Bible*—a book designed for beginner and intermediate musicians looking to understand, improve, and experiment with chords. In this book, you can explore new and exciting sounds that you may have come across in existing pieces of music, or simply add to your repertoire for performing and composing. This is a great reference book that you can go to when you find a chord in a piece of music that you haven't met before.

There are so many possible chords that can be formed on the piano keyboard and to include them all would make this book very long, complicated, and dense. Therefore, I have chosen chords that are most commonly used at a beginner to intermediate level, and found in a variety of musical genres. The chords are arranged in their root key for easy reference, and then divided into four groups: 2-, 3-, 4-, and 5-note chords. Each group covers the chords most common to Western music.

I hope you have a great time exploring these chords and that you will continue to build your repertoire of useful sounds.

Paul Lennon
www.paullennon.com

About this book

1   Chapter title
This letter indicates which note every chord in this chapter will be built upon. You'll find 2-, 3-, 4-, and 5-note chords represented in each chapter and many of them will be in different note arrangements.

2   Introduction
Here you'll find mention of songs or pieces from the classical to modern era in many different styles such as jazz, pop, rock, and country. Use of certain chords within the chapter will be indicated, as well as interesting musical facts.

3   Chord name
Each chord is named clearly, and any other names that you are likely to meet will be found in the Nomenclature guide on page 253.

4   Chord inversions
The inversion of the chord is indicated here to give you a different arrangement of the notes, and therefore a different sound (see Inverting chords on page 10).

5   Middle C
On each keyboard picture, you will notice that one of the white notes is grayed out. This is to indicate where middle C is and provides a fixed point for you to build each chord from.

6   Fingering
A suggested fingering pattern is given for each chord with circles in red for the right hand and in blue for the left hand. The thumb is indicated with a 1 in each hand and then 2, 3, 4, and 5 for the fingers.

1 Chapter title

2 Introduction

3 Chord name

4 Chord inversions

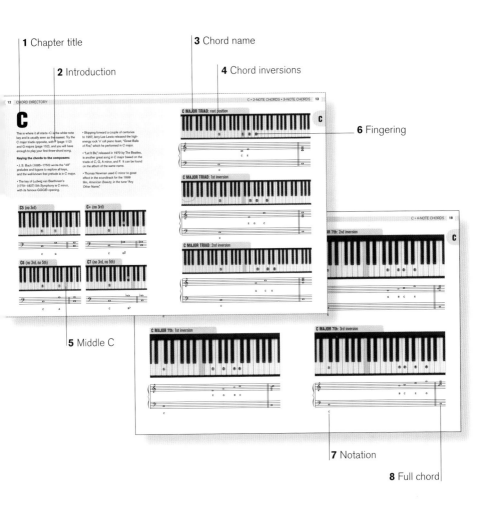

6 Fingering

5 Middle C

7 Notation

8 Full chord

7 Notation

The musical notation for each chord is given below the keyboard and each finger position lines up with the note on the stave. The letter-name for each note is also indicated below the stave.

8 Full chord

At the end of each line of notation, you will find all the notes of the chord written out vertically, one above the other. This is how the chord is to be played and how it will look in a piece of music.

Getting started

Find yourself a keyboard or piano, get comfortable, and begin playing your first basic 2-note chord. When you've mastered this, move on to "triads" and "7th" chords, and begin creating your first chord sequences.

First, find yourself a keyboard...
...Next, sit centrally to the keyboard at the correct height—thighs and forearms should be roughly horizontal. Keep your feet flat on the floor and stay relaxed, with your back straight and shoulders down...
...Then, keeping your wrists flat and curving your fingers, touch the keys with the pads of your fingers; thumbs with the side of the pad. Long fingernails clatter on the keys and can upset the correct hand position so keep them short! Finally, using the diagrams and notation throughout the directory, identify the correct notes with the correct fingers. Play each note separately, then lift your hand off the keys and play all notes together. Repeat the process until you feel comfortable and confident. Now work your way through the chord's inversions.

Correct hand position
The correct hand position involves your fingers, wrists, arms, and all your body. Fingers should be curved—a good reference is to put your hands on your knees when you are sitting at the keyboard, and to keep them in this shape when playing.

A note on fingering

The fingering given for any of the chords is a suggestion only and these may need to change according to context. If you find the fingering awkward for your hand size or hand shape, just experiment until you find something that works. The 3rd and 4th fingers are likely to be the most interchangeable.

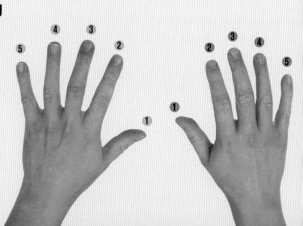

Step one: 2-note chords

Beginner's start here! Every key in this book opens with four basic 2-note chords, that will introduce you to the flavor of the key. Because 2-note chords are played in the left hand only, they are extremely easy to play and can create great backing for many simple tunes. Use C5 (no 3rd), C6 (no 3rd, no 5th), and C7 (no 3rd, no 5th) for a simple blues, and try C5 (no 3rd), C+ (no 3rd), and C6 (no 3rd, no 5th) for a "Latin" sound.

C5 (no 3rd), page 12
Play all 2-note chords with your left hand, using your little finger and thumb.

Step two: 3-note chords

When you think you've mastered the 2-note chords, move on to the 3-note chords, or "triads." Triads are the most common chord-type, and are used in all styles of music from classical to rock. In this book, triads are shown in three different positions, called "inversions" (see page 10). Many piano pieces feature these "inversions" of triads and it is the choice of inversion that makes the sound distinctive.

C major triad (root position), page 13
Play C with your thumb, E with your third finger, and G with your little finger.

Step three: 4-note chords

Now, try your hand at 4-note chords. Most often called 7th chords, these chords are built with 1st, 3rd, 5th, and 7th notes of scales and have a more complex or richer sound. You'll find them in soul, blues, jazz, and classical music and they are principally built from the major and harmonic minor scales—two of the most common scales in Western music. In this book, four of the types—Major 7th, Minor 7th, Dominant 7th, and Minor 7th (♭5)—are given in their different inversions, just like the triads.

C dominant 7th (root position), page 22
The "7th" (B♭) contains dissonance, which means the chord needs to resolve, creating tension and movement.

Want more?

At the end of every section, you will find four examples of **5-note chords** to give you an introduction to the richness of sounds that you can get by adding more notes from the scale—these can be used to spice up chord sequences that may be a little bland.

Chords–the inside track

Before you begin to play the chords in this book, it is important that
you understand how they are built. Once you've got the hang of this
basic theory, you will be able to experiment, discover new sounds,
and even begin composing your own songs.

Building chords

There are four basic scales: major, harmonic
minor, melodic minor, and natural minor. Most
Western music is based on the major/minor
scale system. These scales have seven notes
in semitone and tone steps ranged over all
octaves, as indicated in the diagram on page 11.

Chords are built in thirds. This means that
every other note from a given scale is played
together to create a whole sound. Triads (3-note
chords) are built from note 1, note 3, and note 5;
4-note chords from notes 1, 3, 5, and 7.

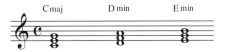

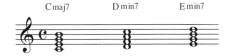

In music notation, chords are stacked vertically on the stave—
in clusters of three for 3-note chords (top), and in groups of
four for 4-note chords (bottom).

As the above diagram indicates, an entire scale can be stacked vertically—1, 3, 5, 7, 9, 11, 13, and 15.
5-note chords are drawn from the higher numbers but always include 1, 3, and 7. This numbering will
help you to distinguish the different ways that notes can be altered to make particular chord sounds.

Inverting chords

From 3-note chords upwards, notes are stacked 1, 3, 5 (or 1, 4, 5 for suspended 4 chords).
These are all as close together as they can be. They can, however, be rearranged vertically,
and this is called "inverting" the chord. Put simply, the bottom note is put on the top—in the
case of 3- and 4-note chords this means putting the bottom note up an octave. In a triad,
C E G becomes E G C. A 4-note chord works the same way: C E G B becomes E G B C.
The first instance of a chord is called "root position" and the subsequent inversions are
numbered "1st inversion," "2nd inversion," and so on. By working through a chord's
inversions, you will extend your repertoire of sounds. Try the C major triad chords on page
13 to get a feel for inversions, and the different sounds they make.

Naming chords

S = semitone
T = tone

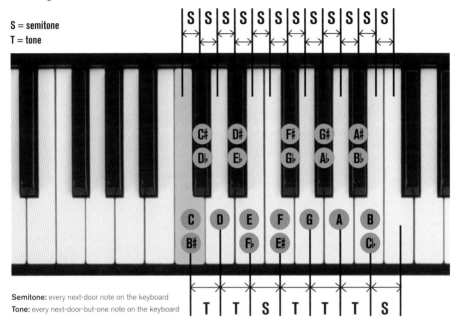

Semitone: every next-door note on the keyboard
Tone: every next-door-but-one note on the keyboard

When a note shares two different names—C♯ and D♭—it is called an "enharmonic." These notes are written and named differently but sound exactly the same. Enharmonic variants have been used throughout this book where it makes the chord easier to read. The diagram above shows all enharmonic notes and where they fall on the keyboard. You will also find this on the quick-reference fold-out flap, which falls on page 253.

Defining chord types

Major: chord with a major 3rd and perfect 5th
Minor: chord with a minor 3rd and perfect 5th
Diminished: chord with a lowered 5th
Augmented: chord with a raised 5th
Dominant: chord built on the 5th note of the major or minor scale
Suspended: chord with a raised 3rd (from major 3rd)

For more on chord types and chord names, see the Nomenclature guide on page 253.

C

This is where it all starts—C is the white-note key and is usually seen as the easiest. Try the C major triads opposite, with F (page 112) and G majors (page 152), and you will have enough to play your first three-chord song.

Keying the chords to the composers:

• J. S. Bach (1685–1750) wrote the "48" preludes and fugues to explore all keys, and the well-known first prelude is in C major.

• The key of Ludwig van Beethoven's (1770–1827) 5th Symphony is C minor, with its famous GGGE♭ opening.

• Skipping forward a couple of centuries to 1957, Jerry Lee Lewis released the high-energy rock 'n' roll piano feast "Great Balls of Fire," which he performed in C major.

• "Let It Be," released in 1970 by The Beatles, is another great song in C major based on the triads of C, G, A minor, and F. It can be found on the album of the same name.

• Thomas Newman used C minor to great effect in the soundtrack for the 1999 film *American Beauty*, in the tune "Any Other Name."

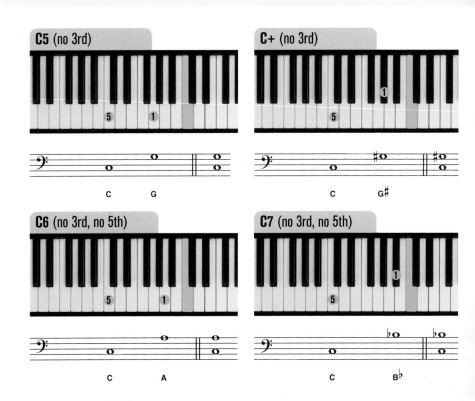

C5 (no 3rd)

C+ (no 3rd)

C6 (no 3rd, no 5th)

C7 (no 3rd, no 5th)

Note: Every good Boy deserves Fudge
EGBDF
FACE

C

C MAJOR TRIAD: root position

C   E   G

c

C MAJOR TRIAD: 1st inversion

E   G   C

c

C MAJOR TRIAD: 2nd inversion

G   C   E

c

C

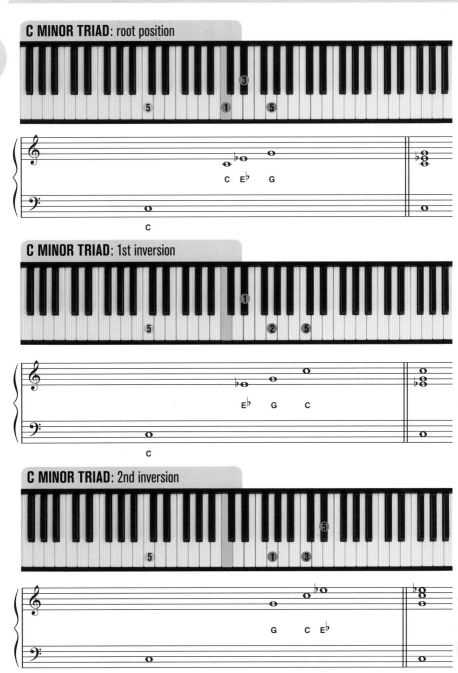

C MINOR TRIAD: root position

C E♭ G

c

C MINOR TRIAD: 1st inversion

E♭ G C

c

C MINOR TRIAD: 2nd inversion

G C E♭

c

C

C DIMINISHED TRIAD: root position

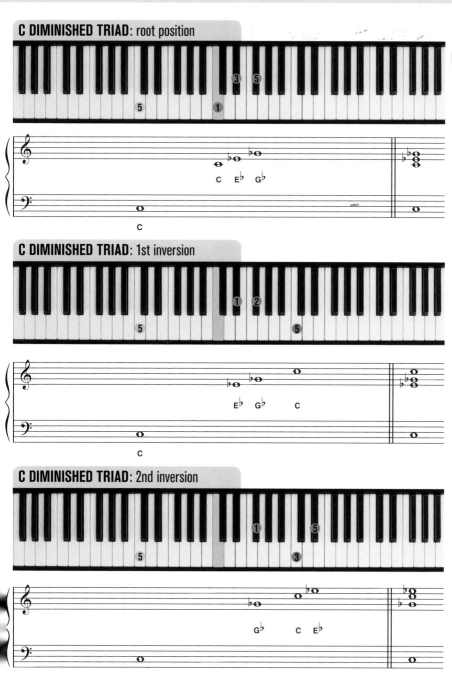

C E♭ G♭

c

C DIMINISHED TRIAD: 1st inversion

E♭ G♭ C

c

C DIMINISHED TRIAD: 2nd inversion

G♭ C E♭

c

C

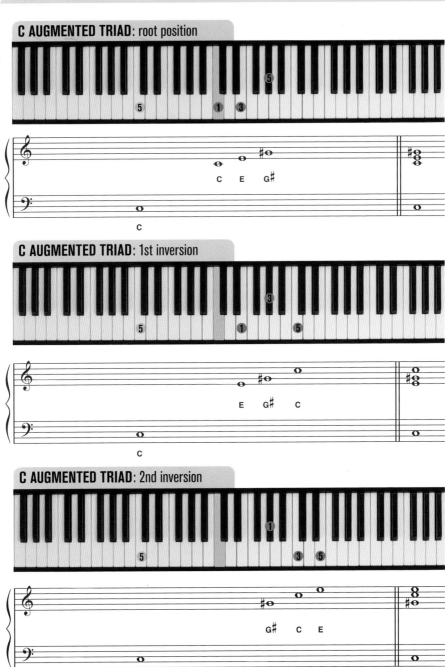

C AUGMENTED TRIAD: root position

C E G#

C

C AUGMENTED TRIAD: 1st inversion

E G# C

C

C AUGMENTED TRIAD: 2nd inversion

G# C E

C

C SUS 4 TRIAD: root position

C SUS 4 TRIAD: 1st inversion

C SUS 4 TRIAD: 2nd inversion

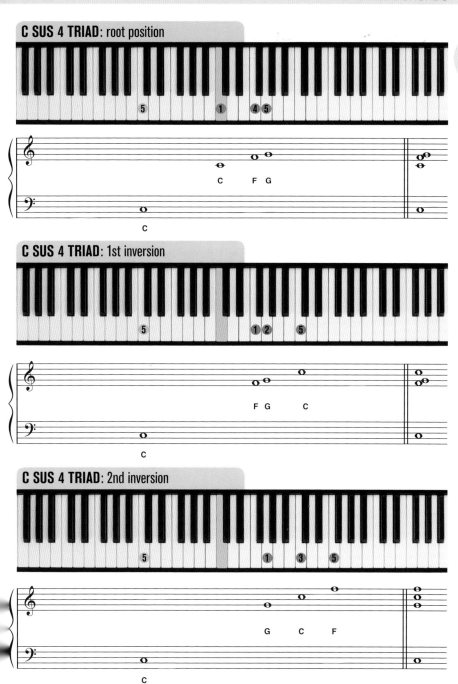

C

C

C MAJOR 7th: root position

C E G B

C

C MAJOR 7th: 1st inversion

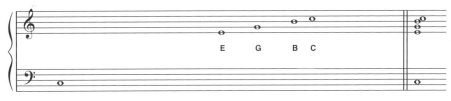

E G B C

C

C

C MAJOR 7th: 2nd inversion

G   B   C   E

C

C MAJOR 7th: 3rd inversion

B   C   E   G

C

C MINOR 7th: root position

C   E♭   G   B♭

C

C MINOR 7th: 1st inversion

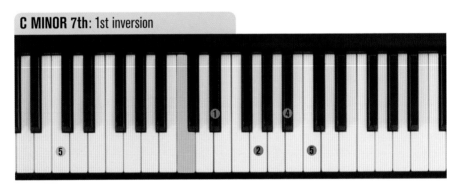

E♭   G   B♭   C

C

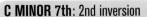

C MINOR 7th: 2nd inversion

G B♭ C E♭

c

C MINOR 7th: 3rd inversion

B♭ C E♭ G

c

C

C DOMINANT 7th: root position

C   E   G   B♭

C

C DOMINANT 7th: 1st inversion

E   G   B♭   C

C

C

C DOMINANT 7th: 2nd inversion

G   B♭   C   E

C

C DOMINANT 7th: 3rd inversion

B♭   C   E   G

C

C

C MINOR 7th (♭5): root position

C   E♭   G♭   B♭

c

C MINOR 7th (♭5): 1st inversion

E♭   G♭   B♭   C

c

C MINOR 7th (♭5): 2nd inversion

G♭ B♭ C E♭

C

C MINOR 7th (♭5): 3rd inversion

B♭ C E♭ G♭

C

C

C DIMINISHED 7th: root position

C E♭ G♭ B♭♭

C

C MAJOR 7th (#5): root position

C E G♯ B

C

C MINOR (MAJOR) 7th: root position

C E♭ G B

C

C MAJOR 7th (#11): root position

C E F# B

C

C

C MAJOR 6th: root position

C E G A

C

C MINOR 6th: root position

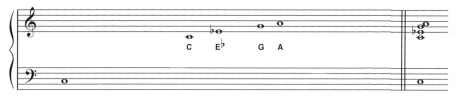

C E♭ G A

C

C DOMINANT 7th SUS 4: root position

C   F   G   B♭

C

C DOMINANT 7th (#11): root position

C   E   F#   B♭

C

C

C DOMINANT 9th: root position

E G B♭ D

C

C DOMINANT 7th (♭9): root position

E G B♭ D♭

C

C

C DOMINANT 13th: root position

C
Bb D E A

C DOMINANT 7th (#9, b13): root position

C
E Ab Bb Eb

C♯/D♭

This key presents you with the first of the enharmonic names (see page 11 for more). From here on in you will meet many chords that have at least two pitch names. Chords occur in all sorts of places within compositions and very often the context will determine how that chord is named, or it may just be easier for the composer to write it that way!

Keying the chords to the composers:

• Frédéric Chopin (1810–1849) wrote his "Minute" Waltz Op.4, No.1 in D♭ major—you will find 2nd inversion D♭ major triads in the left-hand part in the fifth bar of the piece.

• Claude Debussy's (1862–1918) "Claire De Lune" is an impressionist piece in D♭ major and opens with a 1st inversion D♭ major chord, like the one opposite. This piece is found in his 1890 "Suite Bergamasque," and is one of Debussy's most popular piano compositions, along with the Preludes of 1910.

• "Mellon Collie And The Infinite Sadness" by The Smashing Pumpkins, from the 1995 double album of the same name, uses D♭ major triads with E♭ minor (page 72), G♭ (page 132) and B major (page 232) triads in this simple, beautiful piece.

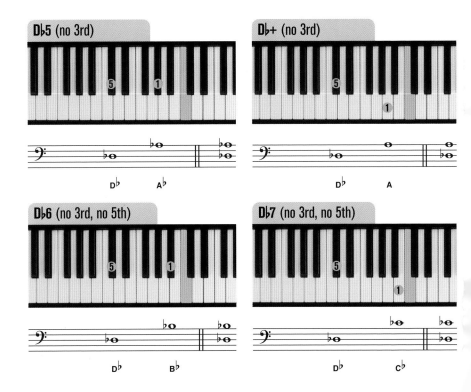

D♭ MAJOR TRIAD: root position

D♭   F   A♭

D♭

D♭ MAJOR TRIAD: 1st inversion

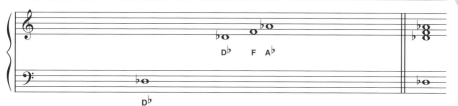

F   A♭   D♭

D♭

D♭ MAJOR TRIAD: 2nd inversion

A♭   D♭   F

D♭

C♯

C♯ MINOR TRIAD: root position

C♯ E G♯

c♯

C♯ MINOR TRIAD: 1st inversion

E G♯ C♯

c♯

C♯ MINOR TRIAD: 2nd inversion

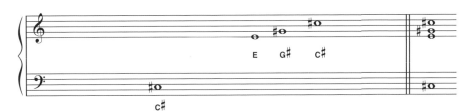

G♯ C♯ E

c♯

C#

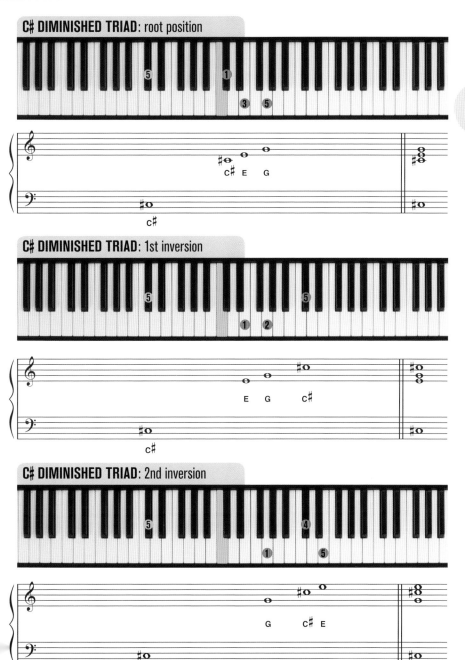

C# DIMINISHED TRIAD: root position

C# E G

c#

C# DIMINISHED TRIAD: 1st inversion

E G c#

c#

C# DIMINISHED TRIAD: 2nd inversion

G c# E

c#

C#

Db AUGMENTED TRIAD: root position

Db AUGMENTED TRIAD: 1st inversion

Db AUGMENTED TRIAD: 2nd inversion

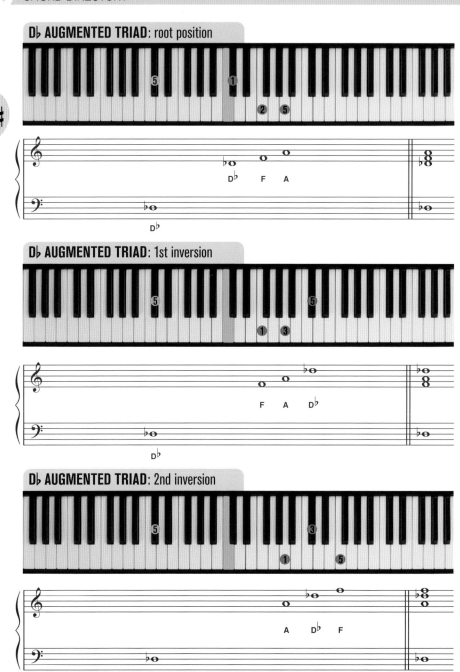

C#

D♭ SUS 4 TRIAD: root position

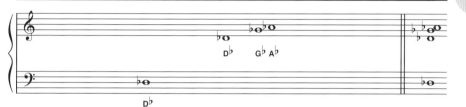

D♭   G♭ A♭

D♭

D♭ SUS 4 TRIAD: 1st inversion

G♭ A♭   D♭

D♭

D♭ SUS 4 TRIAD: 2nd inversion

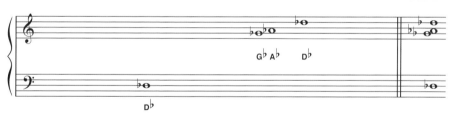

A♭   D♭   G♭

D♭

D♭ MAJOR 7th: root position

D♭   F   A♭   C

D♭

D♭ MAJOR 7th: 1st inversion

F   A♭   C D♭

D♭

D♭ MAJOR 7th: 2nd inversion

A♭   C D♭   F

D♭

D♭ MAJOR 7th: 3rd inversion

C D♭   F   A♭

D♭

C♯ MINOR 7th: root position

C♯ E G♯ B

c♯

C♯ MINOR 7th: 1st inversion

E G♯ B C♯

c♯

C#

C# MINOR 7th: 2nd inversion

G#   B   C#   E

c#

C# MINOR 7th: 3rd inversion

B   C#   E   G#

c#

C#

C# DOMINANT 7th: root position

c# C# E# G# B

C# DOMINANT 7th: 1st inversion

c# E# G# B C#

C# DOMINANT 7th: 2nd inversion

G# B C# E#

c#

C# DOMINANT 7th: 3rd inversion

B C# E# G#

c#

C#

C#

C# MINOR 7th (♭5): root position

C#   E   G   B

c

C# MINOR 7th (♭5): 1st inversion

E   G   B   C#

c#

C# MINOR 7th (♭5): 2nd inversion

G　B　C#　E

c#

C# MINOR 7th (♭5): 3rd inversion

B　C#　E　G

c#

C#

C# DIMINISHED 7th: root position

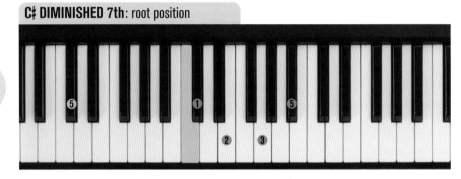

C# E G B♭

c#

D♭ MAJOR 7th (#5): root position

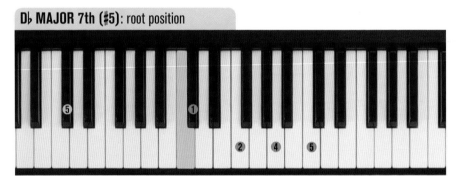

D♭ F A C

D♭

C# MINOR (MAJOR) 7th: root position

C#

C#   E   G#   B#

c#

D♭ MAJOR 7th (#11): root position

D♭   F   G   C

D♭

C#

D♭ MAJOR 6th: root position

D♭   F   A♭   B♭

D♭

C# MINOR 6th: root position

C#   E   G#   A#

c#

C# DOMINANT 7th (SUS 4): root position

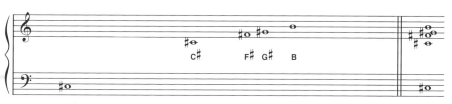

C# F# G# B

c#

D♭ DOMINANT 7th (#11): root position

D♭ F G c♭

D♭

D♭ DOMINANT 9th: root position

F   A♭   C♭   E♭

D♭

C♯ DOMINANT 7th (♭9): root position

E♯   G♯   B   D

C♯

C#

D♭ DOMINANT 13th

C♭   E♭ F   B♭

D♭

C# DOMINANT 7th (#9, ♭13)

E# A B   E

C#

D

This is a very common key for guitars that have their bottom string tuned down to D. Use the D triads with the added octave notes below for a similar open sound. Try adding both major and minor G and A triads (see pages 152 and 192) over D as a static bass note. Keep experimenting with the different inversions to create flowing chord sequences (see Inverting chords on page 10).

Keying the chords to the composers:

• The great Spanish composer Isaac Albeniz (1860–1919) wrote what became a famous tango for solo piano in D major. This piece opens with D major root position triads in the right hand (see page 53).

• "After The Goldrush," a song from the same-titled album released in 1970, in its original form by Neil Young (b.1945), features the D major triads on page 53, along with G, A, and C major, and B minor triads. This song is based around the piano part.

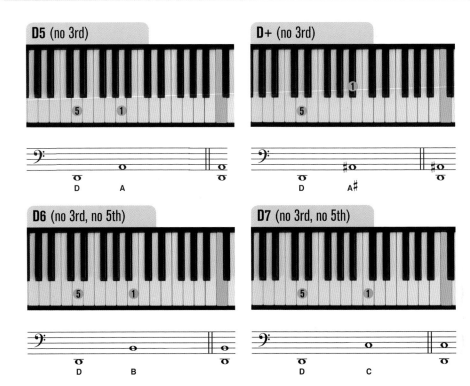

D5 (no 3rd)
D   A

D+ (no 3rd)
D   A♯

D6 (no 3rd, no 5th)
D   B

D7 (no 3rd, no 5th)
D   C

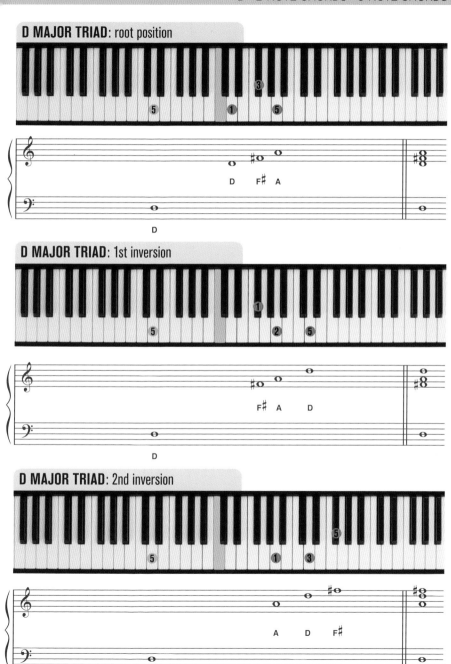

D MAJOR TRIAD: root position

D   F#   A

D

D MAJOR TRIAD: 1st inversion

F#   A   D

D

D MAJOR TRIAD: 2nd inversion

A   D   F#

D

D

D

D MINOR TRIAD: root position

D   F   A

D

D MINOR TRIAD: 1st inversion

F   A   D

D

D MINOR TRIAD: 2nd inversion

A   D   F

D

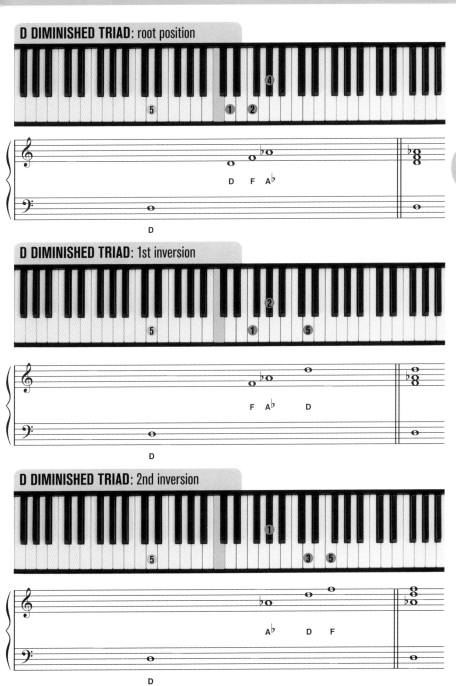

D DIMINISHED TRIAD: root position

D F A♭

D

D DIMINISHED TRIAD: 1st inversion

F A♭ D

D

D DIMINISHED TRIAD: 2nd inversion

A♭ D F

D

D

D AUGMENTED TRIAD: root position

D   F#   A#

D

D AUGMENTED TRIAD: 1st inversion

F#   A#   D

D

D AUGMENTED TRIAD: 2nd inversion

A#   D   F#

D

D

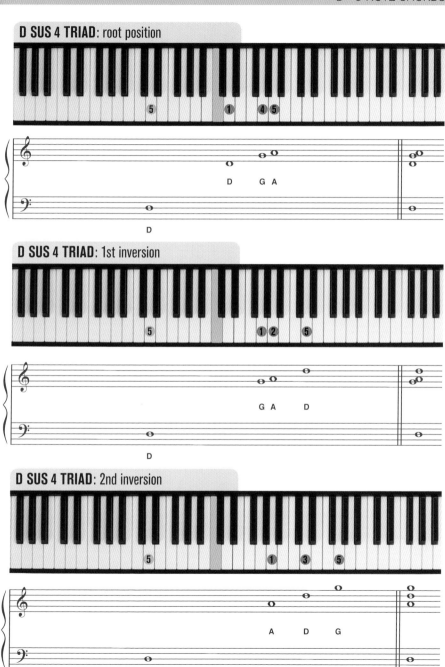

D SUS 4 TRIAD: root position

D G A

D

D SUS 4 TRIAD: 1st inversion

G A D

D

D SUS 4 TRIAD: 2nd inversion

A D G

D

D

D

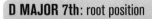

D MAJOR 7th: root position

D   F#   A   C#

D

D MAJOR 7th: 1st inversion

F#   A   C# D

D

D MAJOR 7th: 2nd inversion

A   C♯ D   F♯

D

D

D MAJOR 7th: 3rd inversion

C♯ D   F♯   A

D

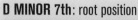

D MINOR 7th: root position

D   F   A   C

D

D MINOR 7th: 1st inversion

F   A   C   D

D

D MINOR 7th: 2nd inversion

A   C   D   F

D

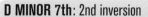

D

D MINOR 7th: 3rd inversion

C   D   F   A

D

D DOMINANT 7th: root position

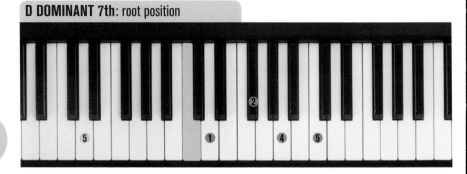

D   F♯   A   C

D

D DOMINANT 7th: 1st inversion

F♯   A   C   D

D

D DOMINANT 7th: 2nd inversion

A   C   D   F#

D

D

D DOMINANT 7th: 3rd inversion

C   D   F#   A

D

D

D MINOR 7th (♭5): root position

D   F   A♭   C

D

D MINOR 7th (♭5): 1st inversion

F   A♭   C   D

D

D MINOR 7th (♭5): 2nd inversion

A♭ C D F

D

D MINOR 7th (♭5): 3rd inversion

C D F A♭

D

D

D DIMINISHED 7th: root position

D   F   A♭   C

D

D MAJOR 7th (♯5): root position

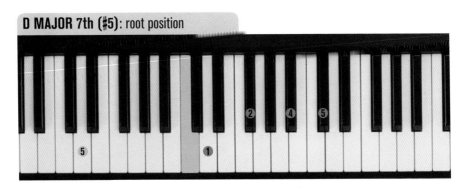

D   F♯   A♯   C♯

D

D MINOR (MAJOR) 7th: root position

D   F   A   C#

D

D MAJOR 7th (#11): root position

D   F#   G#   C#

D

D

D MAJOR 6th: root position

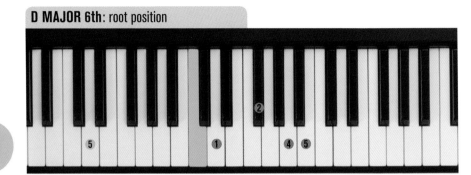

D   F♯   A   B

D

D MINOR 6th: root position

D   F   A   B

D

D DOMINANT 7th (SUS 4): root position

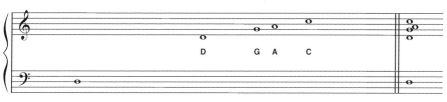

D   G   A   C

D

D

D DOMINANT 7th (#11): root position

D   F#   G#   C

D

D

D DOMINANT 9th: root position

F♯   A   C   E

D

D DOMINANT 7th (♭9): root position

F♯   A   C   E♭

D

D DOMINANT 13th

C   E   F#   B

D

D DOMINANT 7th (#9, ♭13)

F#   B♭   C   F

D

Eb/D#

Rock and metal guitar players often tune their entire instruments down a semitone to Eb, so learning Eb and related chords will be very useful if you find yourself playing with this style of player. You will also find many jazz tunes written for alto saxophone in Eb, mainly from the 1940s and 1950s. These tunes use mostly 7th chords which you will meet on page 78.

Keying the chords to the composers:

• In the 1970s, the singer-songwriter Elton John wrote "Your Song." This is in the key of Eb major with much use of Eb, Ab, and Bb triads in his piano part.

• "Clocks," a piano-dominated song from Coldplay's second album *A Rush Of Blood To The Head* (2002), opens with the Eb major 1st inversion triad on page 73, and is followed by Bb minor 2nd inversion (page 234) and F minor root position (page 114) triads.

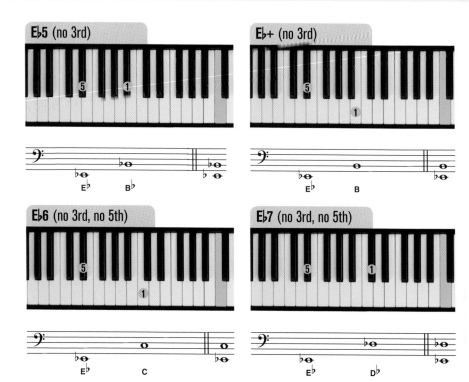

Eb5 (no 3rd)   Eb   Bb

Eb+ (no 3rd)   Eb   B

Eb6 (no 3rd, no 5th)   Eb   C

Eb7 (no 3rd, no 5th)   Eb   Db

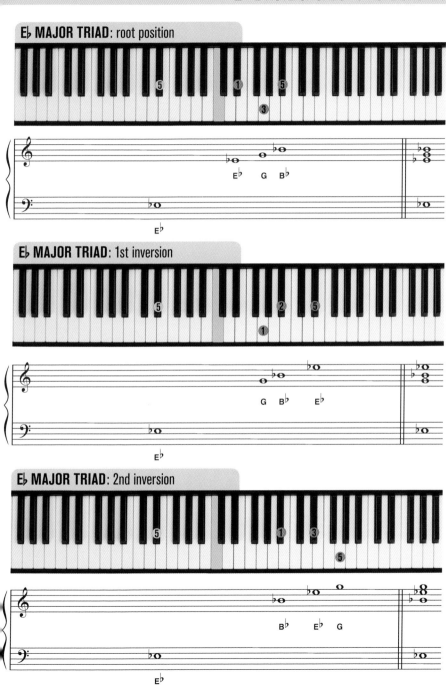

Eb MAJOR TRIAD: root position

Eb G Bb

Eb

Eb

Eb MAJOR TRIAD: 1st inversion

G Bb Eb

Eb

Eb MAJOR TRIAD: 2nd inversion

Bb Eb G

Eb

E♭

E♭ MINOR TRIAD: root position

E♭ G♭ B♭

E♭

E♭ MINOR TRIAD: 1st inversion

G♭ B♭ E♭

E♭

E♭ MINOR TRIAD: 2nd inversion

B♭ E♭ G♭

E♭

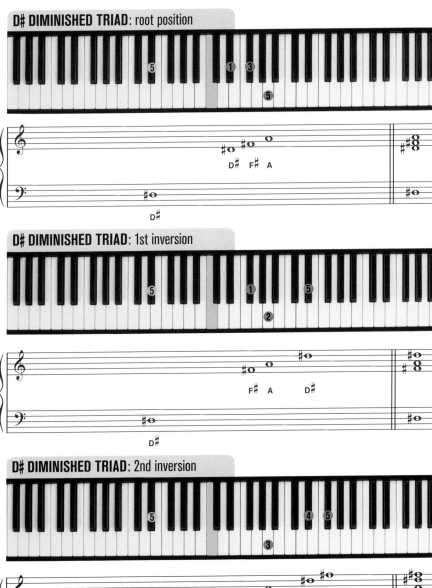

D# DIMINISHED TRIAD: root position

D# F# A

D#

D# DIMINISHED TRIAD: 1st inversion

F# A   D#

D#

D# DIMINISHED TRIAD: 2nd inversion

A   D# F#

D#

E♭

E♭ AUGMENTED TRIAD: root position

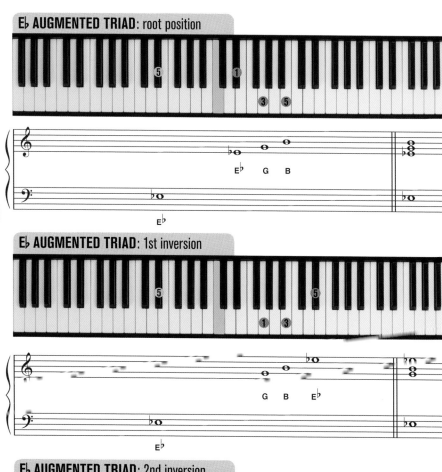

E♭ G B

E♭

E♭ AUGMENTED TRIAD: 1st inversion

G B E♭

E♭

E♭ AUGMENTED TRIAD: 2nd inversion

B E♭ G

E♭

E♭

E♭ SUS 4 TRIAD: root position

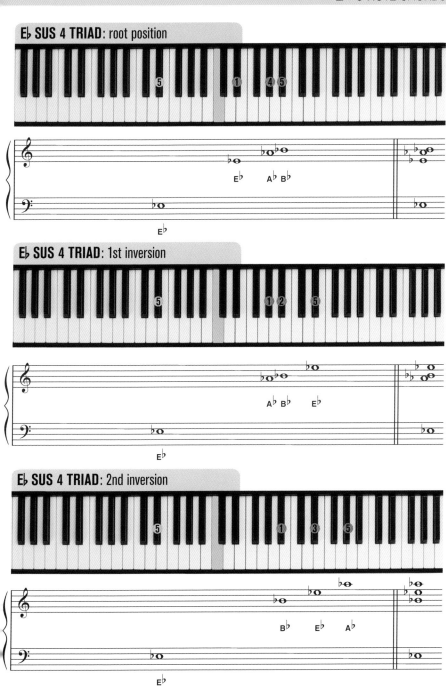

E♭   A♭ B♭

E♭

E♭ SUS 4 TRIAD: 1st inversion

A♭ B♭   E♭

E♭

E♭ SUS 4 TRIAD: 2nd inversion

B♭   E♭   A♭

E♭

E♭

E♭ MAJOR 7th: root position

E♭

E♭   G   B♭   D

E♭

E♭ MAJOR 7th: 1st inversion

G   B♭   D E♭

E♭

Eb MAJOR 7th: 2nd inversion

Bb   D Eb   G

Eb

Eb MAJOR 7th: 3rd inversion

D Eb   G   Bb

Eb

E♭ MINOR 7th: root position

E♭   G♭   B♭   D♭

E♭

E♭ MINOR 7th: 1st inversion

G♭   B♭   D♭   E♭

E♭

Eb MINOR 7th: 2nd inversion

Bb   Db Eb   Gb

Eb

Eb

Eb MINOR 7th: 3rd inversion

Db Eb   Gb   Bb

Eb

E♭ DOMINANT 7th: root position

E♭

E♭   G   B♭   D♭

E♭

E♭ DOMINANT 7th: 1st inversion

G   B♭   D♭   E♭

E♭

Eb DOMINANT 7th: 2nd inversion

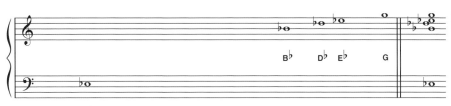

Bb Db Eb G

Eb

Eb DOMINANT 7th: 3rd inversion

Db Eb G Bb

Eb

D# MINOR 7th (♭5): root position

E♭

D#   F#   A   C#

D#

D# MINOR 7th (♭5): 1st inversion

F#   A   C#   D#

D#

D# MINOR 7th (♭5): 2nd inversion

A   C# D#   F#

D#

E♭

D# MINOR 7th (♭5): 3rd inversion

C# D#   F#   A

D#

D♯ DIMINISHED 7th: root position

Eb

D♯   F♯   A   C

D♯

E♭ MAJOR 7th (♯5): root position

E♭   G   B   D

E♭

Eb MINOR (MAJOR) 7th: root position

Eb   Gb   Bb   D

Eb

Eb MAJOR 7th (#11): root position

Eb   G   A   D

Eb

E♭ MAJOR 6th: root position

E♭   G   B♭   C

E♭

E♭

E♭ MINOR 6th: root position

E♭   G♭   B♭   C

E♭

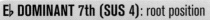

Eb DOMINANT 7th (SUS 4): root position

Eb   Ab Bb   Db

Eb

Eb

Eb DOMINANT 7th (#11): root position

Eb   G A   Db

Eb

E♭ DOMINANT 9th: root position

E♭

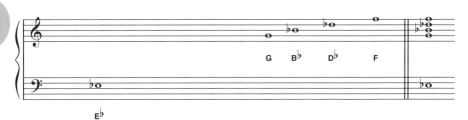

G   B♭   D♭   F

E♭

E♭ DOMINANT 7th (♭9): root position

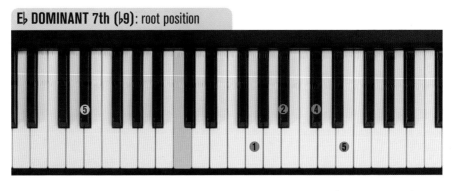

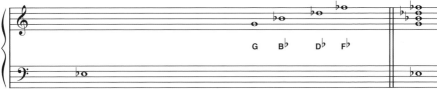

G   B♭   D♭   F♭

E♭

Eb DOMINANT 13th

Eb

Eb DOMINANT 7th (#9, b13)

E

The blues in E is a very common sequence and a very popular one for guitarists. Learn these chords and you will be able to play along with any guitar player. You can use E major, E dominant 7th, and E major 6th chords to build a solid blues sound, along with the same chord-types in A (page 192) and B (page 232).

Keying the chords to the composers:

• In his soundtrack music for the 2001 film *Amélie*, Yann Tiersen used E minor triads in both root position and 1st inversion (listed opposite) in the opening accompaniment for "Comptine D'un Autre Été : L'après-midi."

• The 2006 song "Littlest Things" by Lily Allen from her album *Alright, Still* is a piece in E minor that features piano heavily and uses a repeated 8-bar sequence: E minor, A minor, D, G, E minor, A minor, F♯, and B.

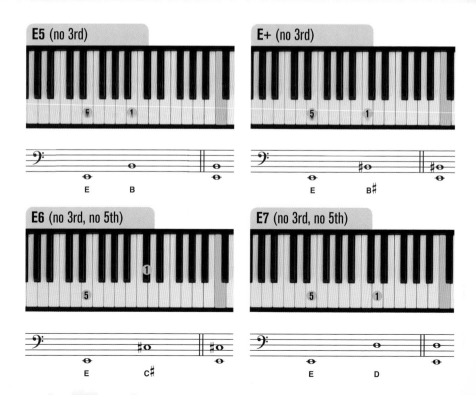

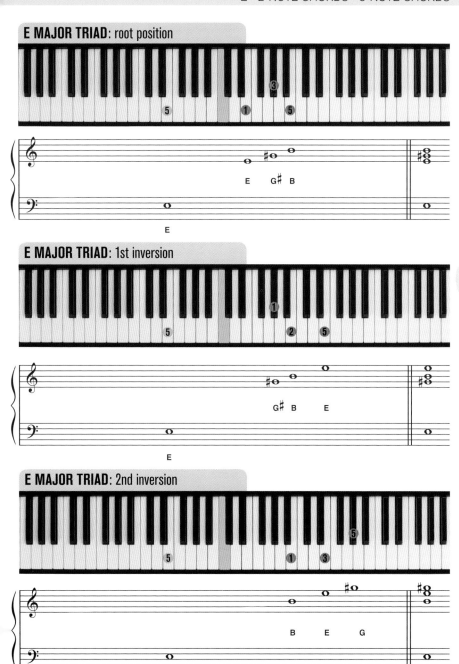

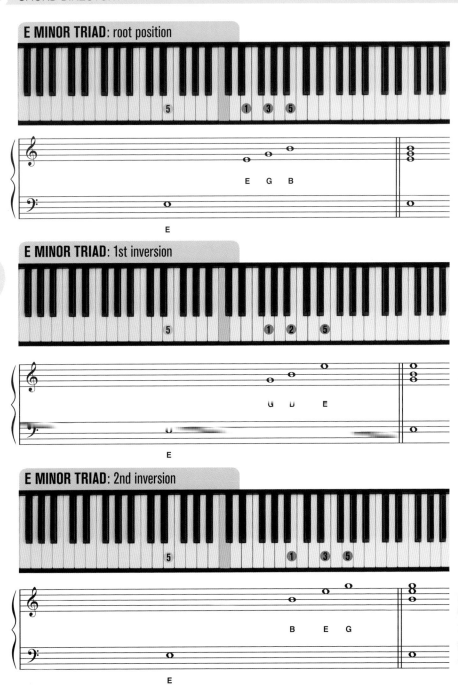

E MINOR TRIAD: root position

E G B

E

E MINOR TRIAD: 1st inversion

G B E

E

E MINOR TRIAD: 2nd inversion

B E G

E

E

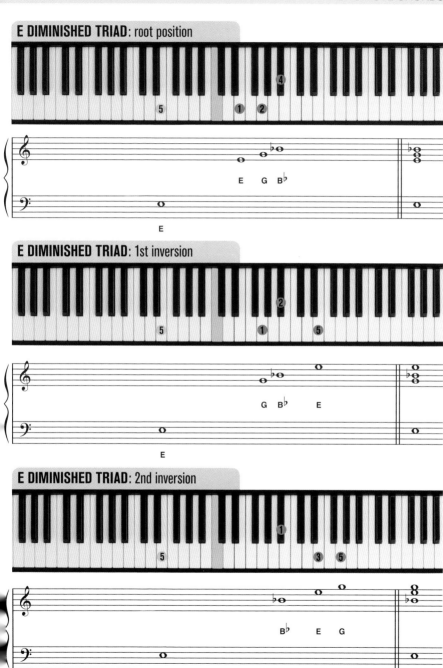

E DIMINISHED TRIAD: root position

E G B♭

E

E DIMINISHED TRIAD: 1st inversion

G B♭ E

E

E DIMINISHED TRIAD: 2nd inversion

B♭ E G

E

E

E AUGMENTED TRIAD: root position

E AUGMENTED TRIAD: 1st inversion

E AUGMENTED TRIAD: 2nd inversion

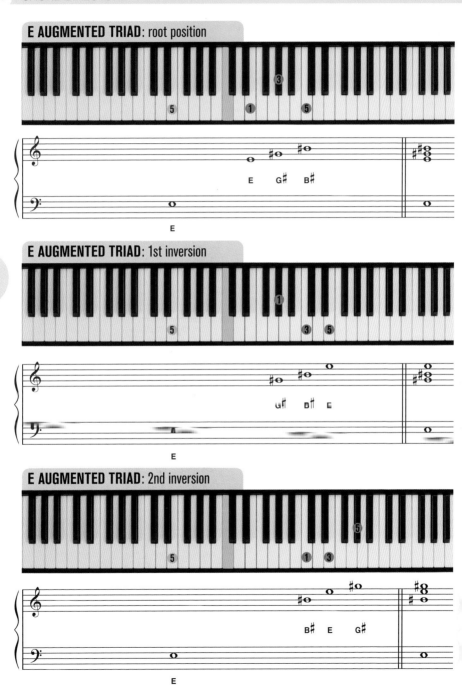

E

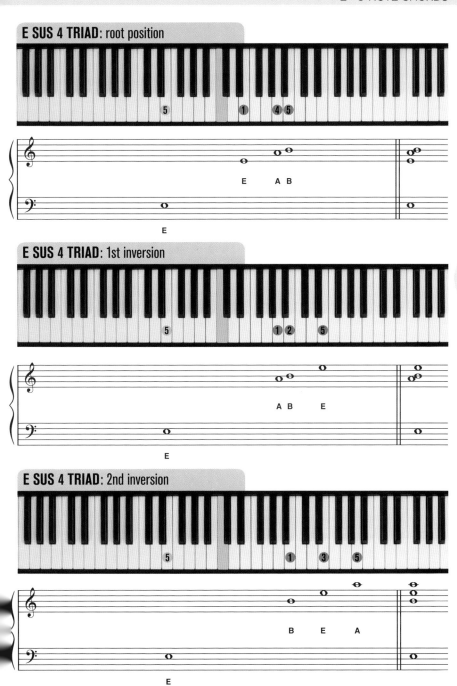

E SUS 4 TRIAD: root position

5   ① ④⑤

E   A B

E

E SUS 4 TRIAD: 1st inversion

5   ①② ⑤

A B   E

E

E SUS 4 TRIAD: 2nd inversion

5   ① ③ ⑤

B E A

E

E

E MAJOR 7th: root position

E   G♯   B   D♯

E

E MAJOR 7th: 1st inversion

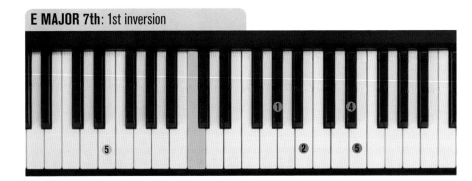

G♯   B   D♯ E

E

E MAJOR 7th: 2nd inversion

B   D♯ E   G♯

E

E MAJOR 7th: 3rd inversion

D♯ E   G♯   B

E

E MINOR 7th: root position

E

E G B D

E

E MINOR 7th: 1st inversion

G B D E

E

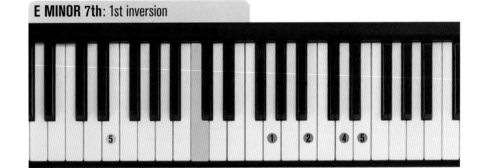

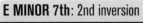

E MINOR 7th: 2nd inversion

B   D E   G

E

E

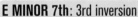

E MINOR 7th: 3rd inversion

D E   G   B

E

E DOMINANT 7th: root position

E   G♯   B   D

E

E

E DOMINANT 7th: 1st inversion

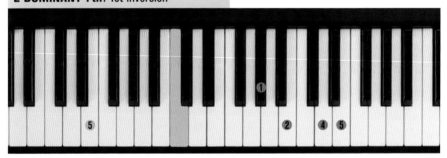

G♯   B   D   E

E

E DOMINANT 7th: 2nd inversion

B   D   E   G♯

E

E

E DOMINANT 7th: 3rd inversion

D   E   G♯   B

E

E

E MINOR 7th (♭5): root position

E   G   B♭   D

E

E MINOR 7th (♭5): 1st inversion

G   B♭   D   E

E

E MINOR 7th (♭5): 2nd inversion

B♭ D E G

E

E MINOR 7th (♭5): 3rd inversion

D E G B♭

E

E DIMINISHED 7th: root position

E   G   B♭   D♭

E

E MAJOR 7th (♯5): root position

E   G♯   B♯   D♯

E

E

E MINOR (MAJOR) 7th: root position

E   G   B   D#

E

E MAJOR 7th (#11): root position

E   G# A#   D#

E

E

E MAJOR 6th: root position

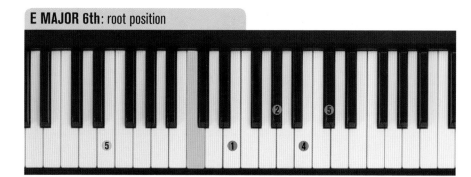

E   G#   B   C#

E

E

E MINOR 6th: root position

E   G   B   C#

E

E DOMINANT 7th (SUS 4): root position

E   A   B   D

E

E DOMINANT 7th (#11): root position

E   G♯ A♯   D

E

E

E

E DOMINANT 9th: root position

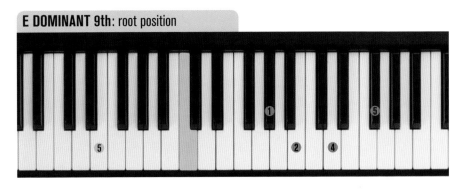

G#   B   D   F#

E

E DOMINANT 7th (♭9): root position

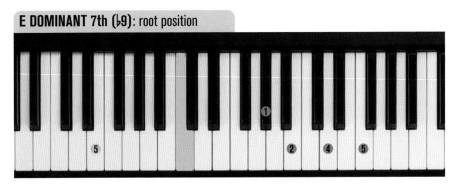

G#   B   D   F

E

E DOMINANT 13th

D   F♯ G♯   C♯

E

E

E DOMINANT 7th (♯9, ♭13)

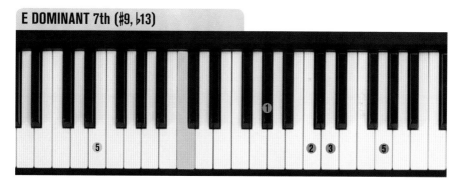

G♯   C D   G

E

F

F is a very common jazz key, and knowing the 12-bar blues in F will be very useful for any "jam" session situation. Use the chords of F, B♭, and C in dominant 7th and major 6th forms to build the blues sequence.

Keying the chords to the composers:

• The romantic composer Robert Schumann (1810–1856) wrote his famous "Träumerei" (Dreaming) for solo piano in F major. It is found in his "Kinderszenen" Op.15, No.7, and was composed in spring 1838. It charms with its simple melody and spacious accompaniment, and is a popular encore for classical pianists.

• In the 1930s and 1940s, Charlie Parker (1920-1955) wrote many blues in F using F7 (page 122), B♭7 (page 222), and C7 chords (page 22). Although he was a saxophone player, his compositions are a useful source for blues and jazz pianists. His famous tunes "Now's The Time," "Blues For Alice," "Billie's Bounce," and "Au Privave" all use the 12-bar blues chord sequence as their basis.

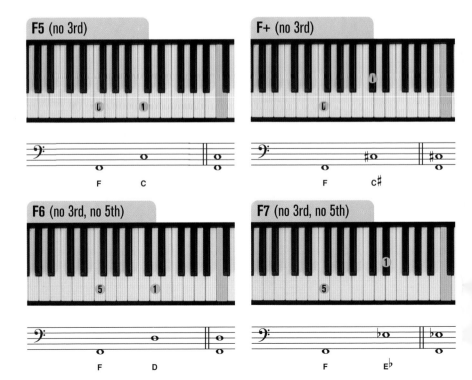

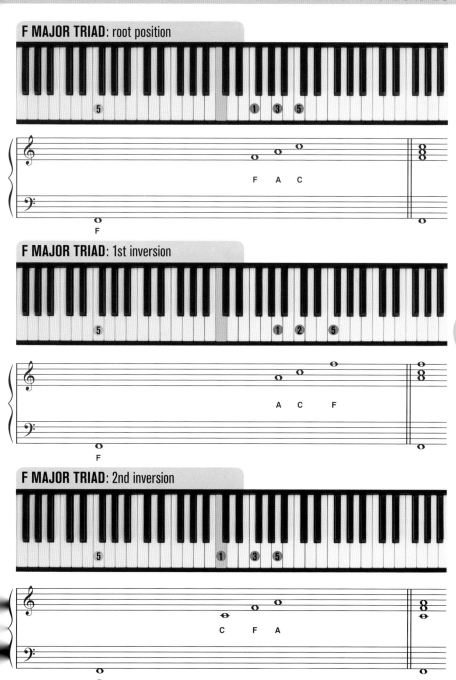

F MAJOR TRIAD: root position

F A C

F

F MAJOR TRIAD: 1st inversion

A C F

F

F

F MAJOR TRIAD: 2nd inversion

C F A

F

F MINOR TRIAD: root position

F A♭ C

F

F MINOR TRIAD: 1st inversion

A♭ C F

F

F MINOR TRIAD: 2nd inversion

C F A♭

F

F

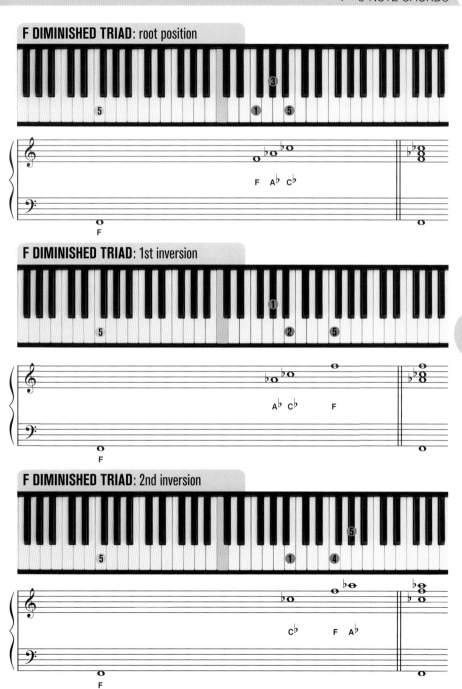

F DIMINISHED TRIAD: root position

F A♭ C♭

F

F DIMINISHED TRIAD: 1st inversion

A♭ C♭ F

F

F DIMINISHED TRIAD: 2nd inversion

C♭ F A♭

F

F AUGMENTED TRIAD: root position

F   A   C#

F

F AUGMENTED TRIAD: 1st inversion

A   C#   F

F

F AUGMENTED TRIAD: 2nd inversion

C#   F   A

F

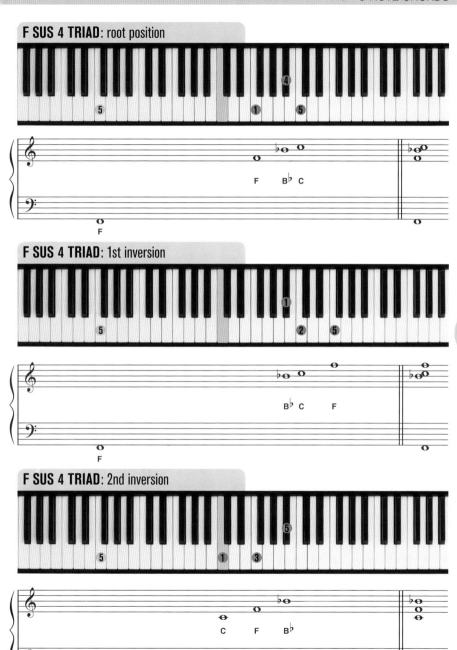

F MAJOR 7th: root position

F A C E

F

F

F MAJOR 7th: 1st inversion

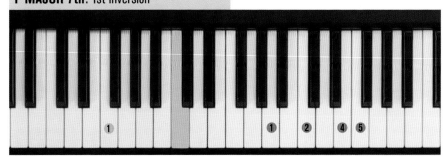

A C E F

F

F MAJOR 7th: 2nd inversion

C   E F   A

F

F

F MAJOR 7th: 3rd inversion

E F   A   C

F

F MINOR 7th: root position

F   A♭   C   E♭

F

F

F MINOR 7th: 1st inversion

A♭   C   E♭   F

F

F MINOR 7th: 2nd inversion

C   E♭   F   A♭

F

F

F MINOR 7th: 3rd inversion

E♭   F   A♭   C

F

F DOMINANT 7th: root position

F   A   C   E♭

F

F

F DOMINANT 7th: 1st inversion

A   C   E♭   F

F

F DOMINANT 7th: 2nd inversion

C E♭ F A

F

F DOMINANT 7th: 3rd inversion

E♭ F A C

F

F MINOR 7th (♭5): root position

F   A♭   C♭   E♭

F

F

F MINOR 7th (♭5): 1st inversion

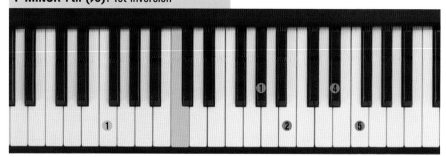

A♭   C♭   E♭   F

F

F MINOR 7th (♭5): 2nd inversion

C♭ E♭ F A♭

F

F

F MINOR 7th (♭5): 3rd inversion

E♭ F A♭ C♭

F

F DIMINISHED 7th: root position

F   A♭   C♭   E♭♭

F

F

F MAJOR 7th (#5): root position

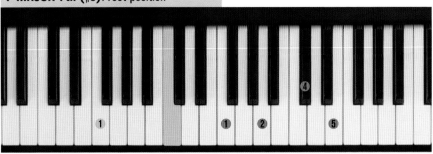

F   A   C#   E

F

F MINOR (MAJOR) 7th: root position

F   A♭   C   E

F

F

F MAJOR 7th (#11): root position

F   A   B   E

F

F MAJOR 6th: root position

F   A   C   D

F

F

F MINOR 6th: root position

F   A♭   C   D

F

F DOMINANT 7th (SUS 4): root position

F   B♭   C   E♭

F

F

F DOMINANT 7th (#11): root position

F   A   B   E♭

F DOMINANT 9th: root position

A C E♭ G

F

F

F DOMINANT 7th (♭9): root position

A C E♭ G♭

F

F DOMINANT 13th

E♭   G   A   D

F

F

F DOMINANT 7th (♯9, ♭13)

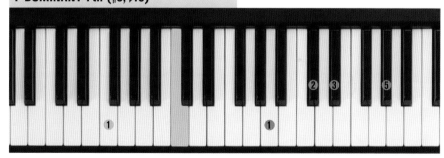

A   D♭ E♭   A♭

F

F#/Gb

The American songwriter Irving Berlin (1888–1989) used mainly the black keys of his piano in his playing and composing, and subsequently wrote many songs in F# major. To be able to transpose to other keys he had a special piano built, which had a lever that could change the key–rather like many modern keyboards do.

Keying the chords to the composers:

• Claude Debussy wrote in certain keys to express particular colors or moods. A good example of this is "The Girl With The Flaxen Hair," which can be found in the first book of Preludes. The wistful character of this piece has much to do with his choice of key–Gb.

• Radiohead's wandering, whimsical single "Pyramid Song," from the 2001 album *Amnesiac*, uses both F# major and minor triads along with G, A, and E major triads. Listen out for the Indian-style strings!

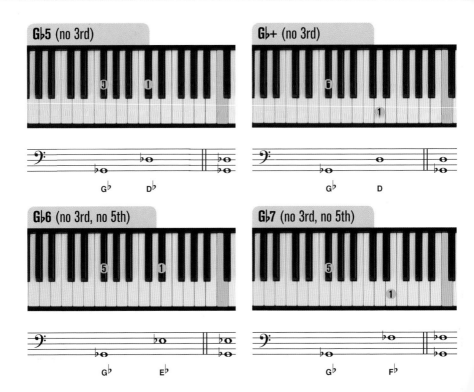

F# MAJOR TRIAD: root position

F# MAJOR TRIAD: 1st inversion

F# MAJOR TRIAD: 2nd inversion

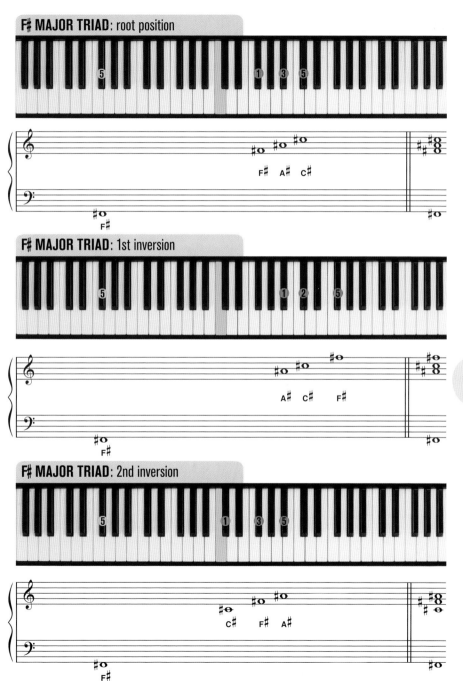

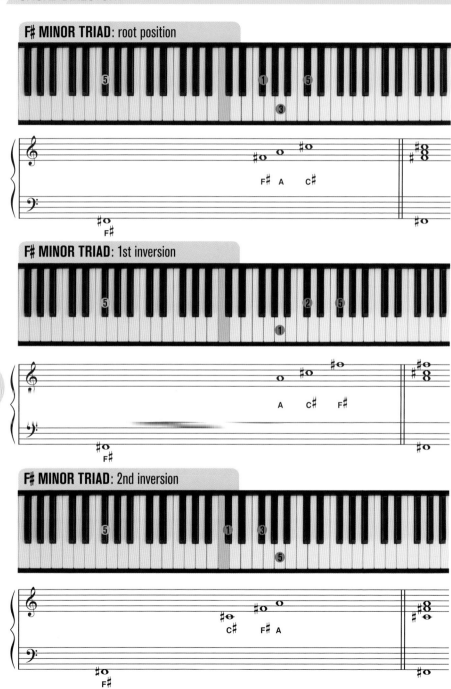

F# MINOR TRIAD: root position

F# A C#

F#

F# MINOR TRIAD: 1st inversion

A C# F#

F#

F#

F# MINOR TRIAD: 2nd inversion

C# F# A

F#

F# DIMINISHED TRIAD: root position

F# DIMINISHED TRIAD: 1st inversion

F# DIMINISHED TRIAD: 2nd inversion

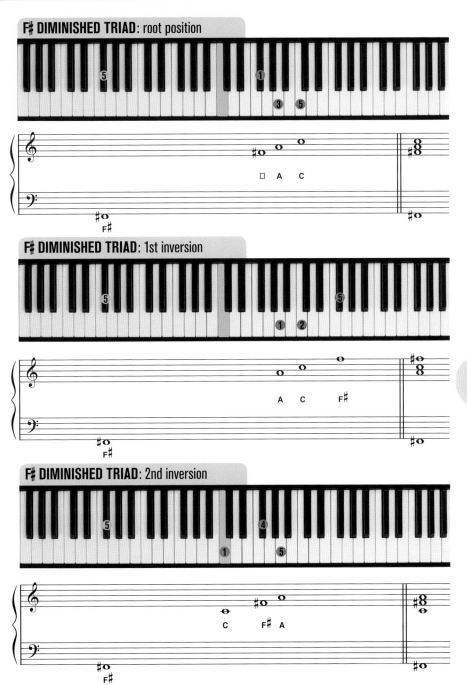

F#

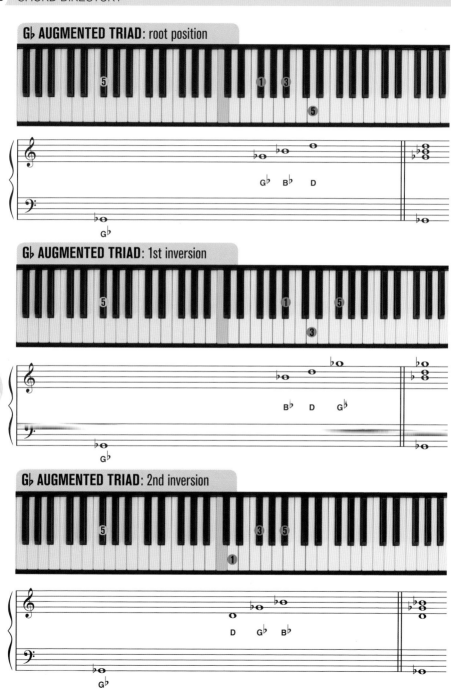

G♭ AUGMENTED TRIAD: root position

G♭   B♭   D

G♭

G♭ AUGMENTED TRIAD: 1st inversion

F♯

B♭   D   G♭

G♭

G♭ AUGMENTED TRIAD: 2nd inversion

D   G♭   B♭

G♭

F# SUS 4 TRIAD: root position

F# SUS 4 TRIAD: 1st inversion

F#

F# SUS 4 TRIAD: 2nd inversion

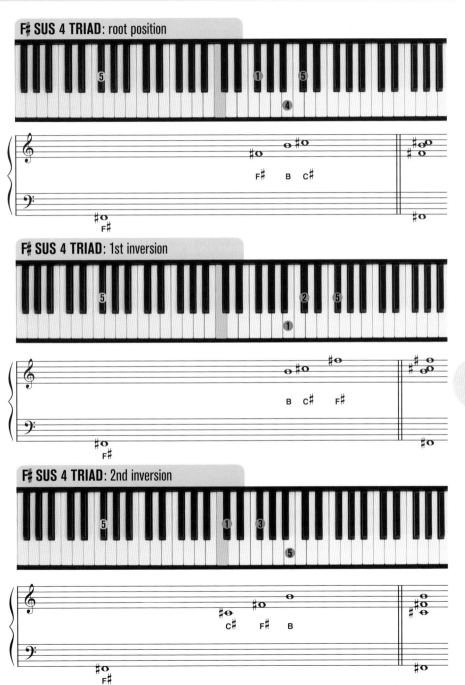

F# MAJOR 7th: root position

F#   A#   C#   E#

F#

F#

F# MAJOR 7th: 1st inversion

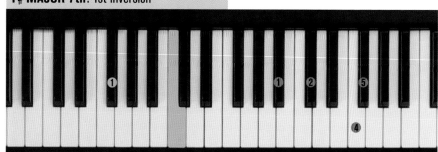

A#   C#   E# F#

F#

F# MAJOR 7th: 2nd inversion

C#   E# F#   A#

F#

F# MAJOR 7th: 3rd inversion

E# F#   A#   C#

F#

F# MINOR 7th: root position

F#   A   C#   E

F#

F#

F# MINOR 7th: 1st inversion

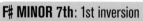

A   C#   E   F#

F#

F# MINOR 7th: 2nd inversion

C# E F# A

F#

F# MINOR 7th: 3rd inversion

F#

E F# A C#

F#

F# DOMINANT 7th: root position

F#   A#   C#   E

F#

F#

F# DOMINANT 7th: 1st inversion

A#   C#   E   F#

F#

F# DOMINANT 7th: 2nd inversion

C# E F# A#

F#

F#

F# DOMINANT 7th: 3rd inversion

E F# A# C#

F#

F# MINOR 7th (♭5): root position

F#   A   C   E

F#

F# MINOR 7th (♭5): 1st inversion

A   C   E   F#

F#

F# MINOR 7th (♭5): 2nd inversion

C   E   F#   A

F#

F# MINOR 7th (♭5): 3rd inversion

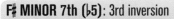

F#

E   F#   A   C

F#

F# DIMINISHED 7th: root position

F#   A   C   E♭

F#

G♭ MAJOR 7th (#5): root position

G♭   B♭   D   F

G♭

F# MINOR (MAJOR) 7th: root position

F#   A   C#   E#

F#

G♭ MAJOR 7th (#11): root position

F#

G♭   B♭   C   F

G♭

G♭ MAJOR 6th: root position

G♭   B♭   D♭   E♭

G♭

F#

F# MINOR 6th: root position

F#   A   C#   D#

F#

F# DOMINANT 7th (SUS 4): root position

F#   B   C#   E

F#

F#

G♭ DOMINANT 7th (#11): root position

G♭   B♭   C   F♭

G♭

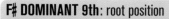

F♯ DOMINANT 9th: root position

A♯ C♯ E G♯

F♯

F♯ DOMINANT 7th (♭9): root position

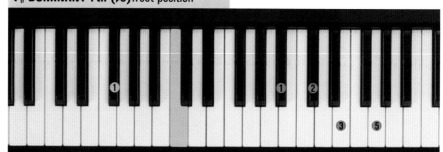

A♯ C♯ E G

F♯

F♯

F♯ DOMINANT 13th

E   G♯ A♯   D♯

F♯

F♯ DOMINANT 7th (#9, ♭13)

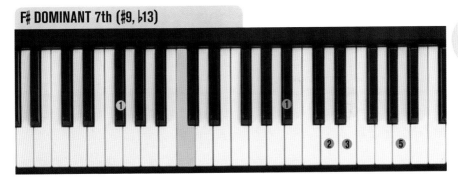

A♯   D E   A

F♯

F♯

Country songs are often written in G major with C, F, A minor, and D minor chords. These are all white-note chords on the keyboard so they are very easy to play–for beginner keyboard players and guitar players alike.

Keying the chords to the composers:

• In his famous Minuet in G, Ludwig van Beethoven (1770–1817) uses G major triads in root position without doubling the bottom note of the triad. The accompanying trio section features broken chords including the root position G major triad and also a D dominant 7th chord in the second bar.

• In 1986, the piano-led band Bruce Hornsby and The Range released the album *The Way It Is*. The title song has a great piano part in G major and uses the 1st inversion triad featured on page 153 in the main piano riff.

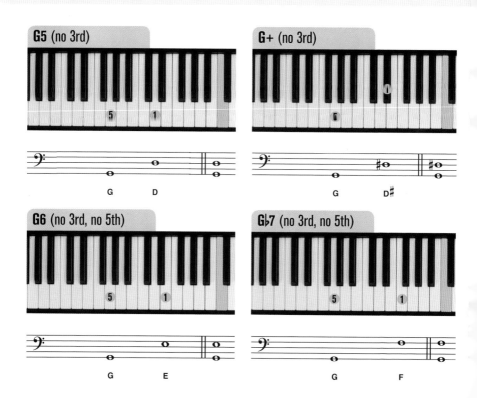

G MAJOR TRIAD: root position

G MAJOR TRIAD: 1st inversion

G MAJOR TRIAD: 2nd inversion

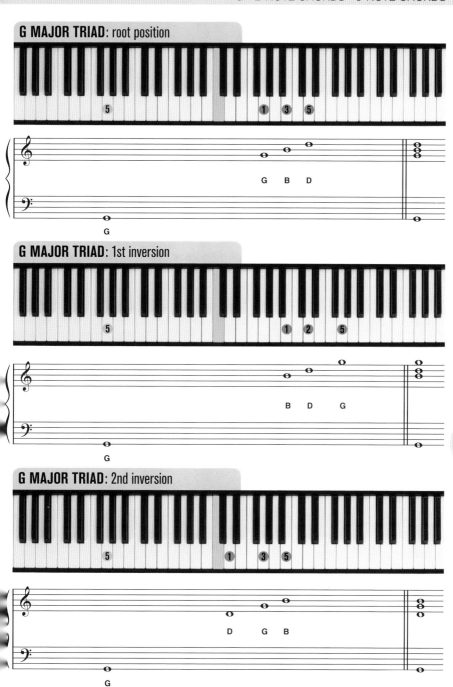

G MINOR TRIAD: root position

G B♭ D

G

G MINOR TRIAD: 1st inversion

B♭ D G

G

G MINOR TRIAD: 2nd inversion

D G B♭

G

G

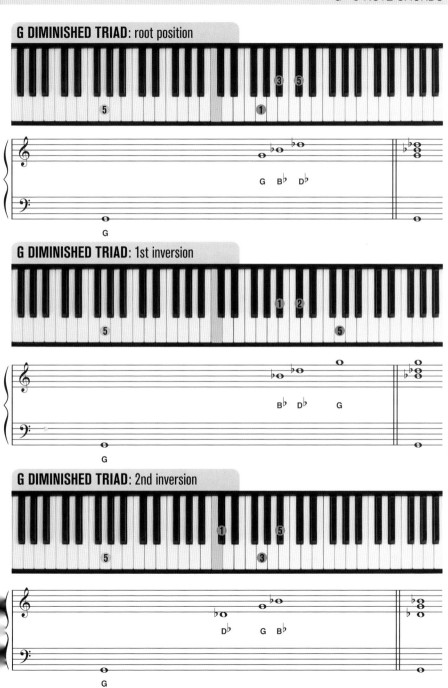

G DIMINISHED TRIAD: root position

G B♭ D♭

G

G DIMINISHED TRIAD: 1st inversion

B♭ D♭ G

G

G DIMINISHED TRIAD: 2nd inversion

D♭ G B♭

G

G

G AUGMENTED TRIAD: root position

G AUGMENTED TRIAD: 1st inversion

G AUGMENTED TRIAD: 2nd inversion

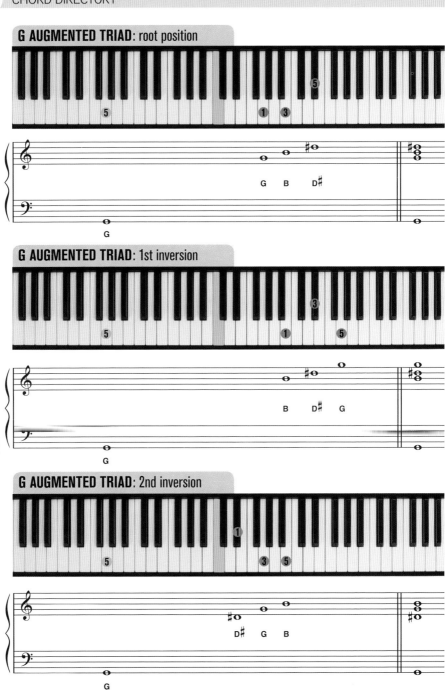

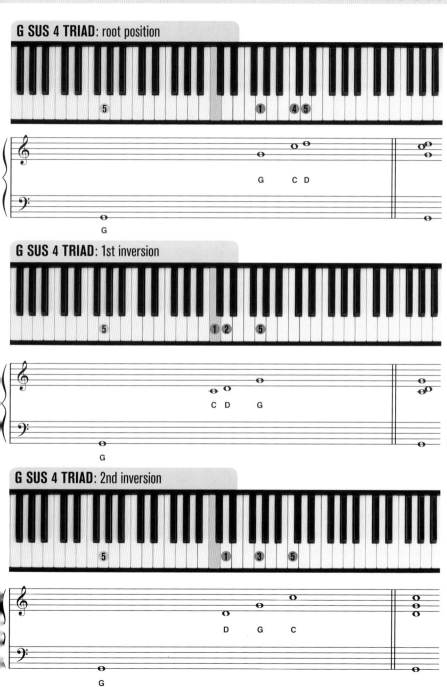

G SUS 4 TRIAD: root position

G SUS 4 TRIAD: 1st inversion

G SUS 4 TRIAD: 2nd inversion

G

G MAJOR 7th: root position

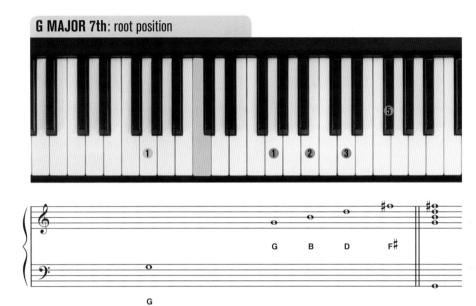

G   B   D   F♯

G

G MAJOR 7th: 1st inversion

G

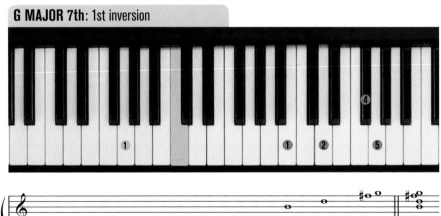

B   D   F♯G

G

G MAJOR 7th: 2nd inversion

D   F♯ G   B

G

G MAJOR 7th: 3rd inversion

F♯ G   B   D

G

G

G MINOR 7th: root position

G   B♭   D   F

G

G MINOR 7th: 1st inversion

B♭   D   F   G

G

G

G MINOR 7th: 2nd inversion

D   F   G   B♭

G

G MINOR 7th: 3rd inversion

F   G   B♭   D

G

G

G DOMINANT 7th: root position

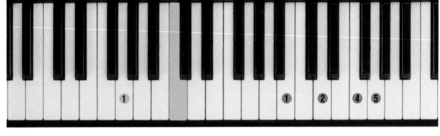

G   B   D   F

G

G DOMINANT 7th: 1st inversion

B   D   F   G

G

G

G DOMINANT 7th: 2nd inversion

D   F G   B

G

G DOMINANT 7th: 3rd inversion

F   G   B   D

G

G

G MINOR 7th (♭5): root position

G   B♭   D♭   F

G

G MINOR 7th (♭5): 1st inversion

G

B♭   D♭   F   G

G

G MINOR 7th (♭5): 2nd inversion

D♭   F   G   B♭

G

G MINOR 7th (♭5): 3rd inversion

G

F   G   B♭   D♭

G

G DIMINISHED 7th: root position

G   B♭   D♭   F♭

G

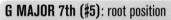

G MAJOR 7th (♯5): root position

G

G   B   D♯   F♯

G

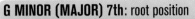

G MINOR (MAJOR) 7th: root position

G   B♭   D   F♯

G

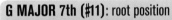

G MAJOR 7th (♯11): root position

G   B   C♯   F♯

G

G

G MAJOR 6th: root position

G B D E

G

G MINOR 6th: root position

G

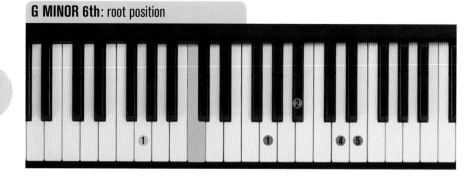

G B♭ D E

G

G DOMINANT 7th (SUS 4): root position

G   C   D   F

G

G DOMINANT 7th (#11): root position

G   B   C#   F

G

G

G DOMINANT 9th: root position

B D F A

G

G

G DOMINANT 7th (♭9): root position

B D F A♭

G

G DOMINANT 13th

F A B E

G

G DOMINANT 7th (#9, ♭13)

B E♭ F B♭

G

G

A♭/G♯

Mixing chords from different keys is very common in most styles of music. As an example, try an A♭ major chord instead of A minor in the key of C. Add a B♭ major to this and you're getting somewhere. This gives a uniquely characteristic sound that can often be found in Gospel and pop music.

Keying the chords to the composers:

• The slow movement of Beethoven's Pathetique Sonata No. 8 in C minor is in A♭ major and features a second inversion A♭ major triad in the right hand (see page 173) with much sixteenth-note movement.

• Scott Joplin (1868–1917) wrote his most famous piano piece "Maple Leaf Rag" in 1899, and this became the first instrumental to sell over a million copies. It's in A♭ major and uses many octaves in the right hand with a stride (bass-note followed by chord) left-hand part. The opening idea is based on the 2nd inversion major triad listed on page 173.

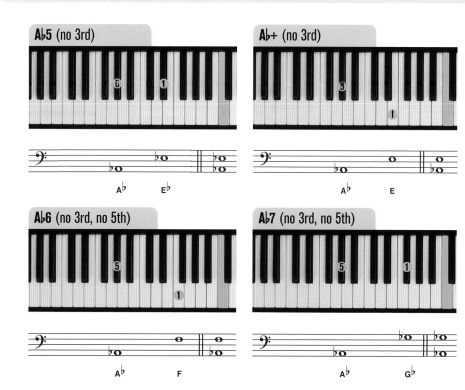

Ab MAJOR TRIAD: root position

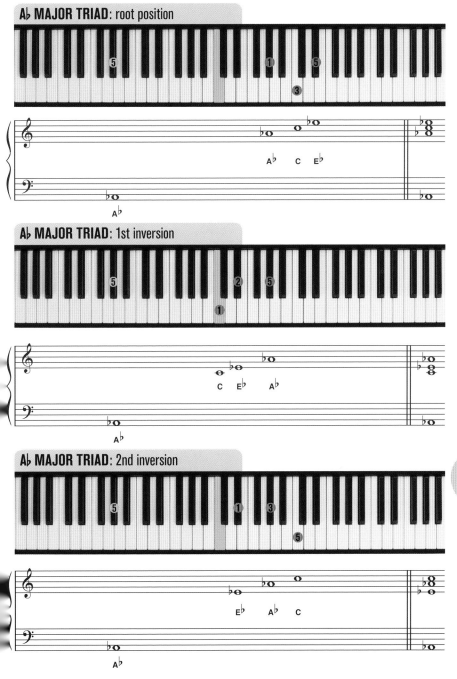

Ab   C   Eb

Ab

Ab MAJOR TRIAD: 1st inversion

C   Eb   Ab

Ab

Ab MAJOR TRIAD: 2nd inversion

Eb   Ab   C

Ab

A♭ MINOR TRIAD: root position

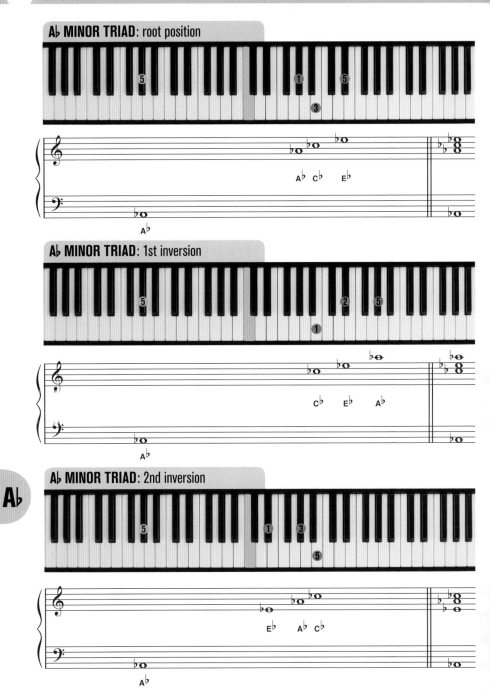

A♭ C♭ E♭

A♭

A♭ MINOR TRIAD: 1st inversion

C♭ E♭ A♭

A♭

A♭

A♭ MINOR TRIAD: 2nd inversion

E♭ A♭ C♭

A♭

G# DIMINISHED TRIAD: root position

G# DIMINISHED TRIAD: 1st inversion

G# DIMINISHED TRIAD: 2nd inversion

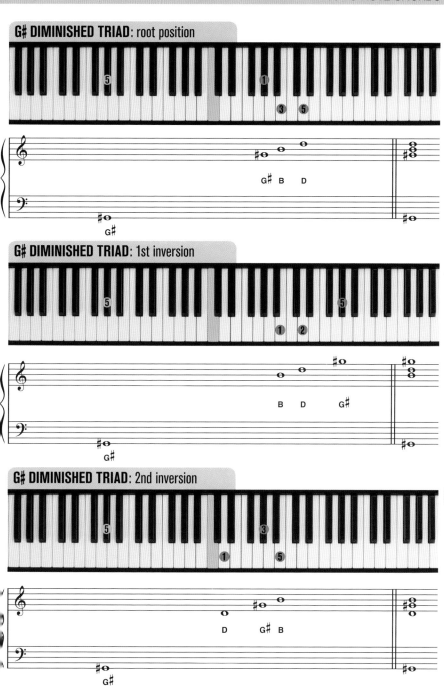

A♭

A♭ AUGMENTED TRIAD: root position

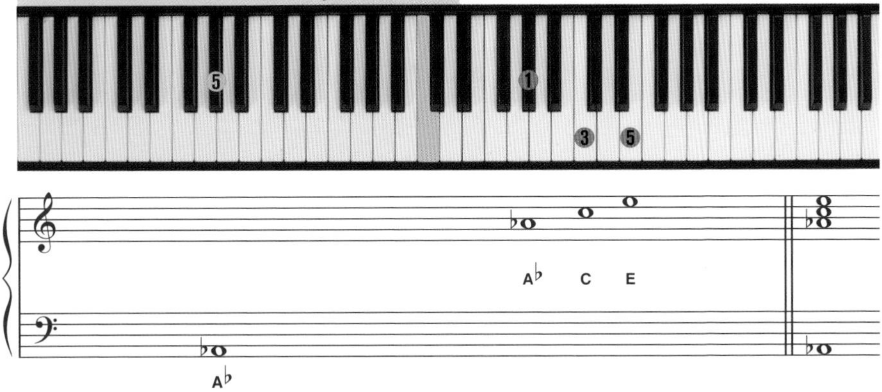

A♭ AUGMENTED TRIAD: 1st inversion

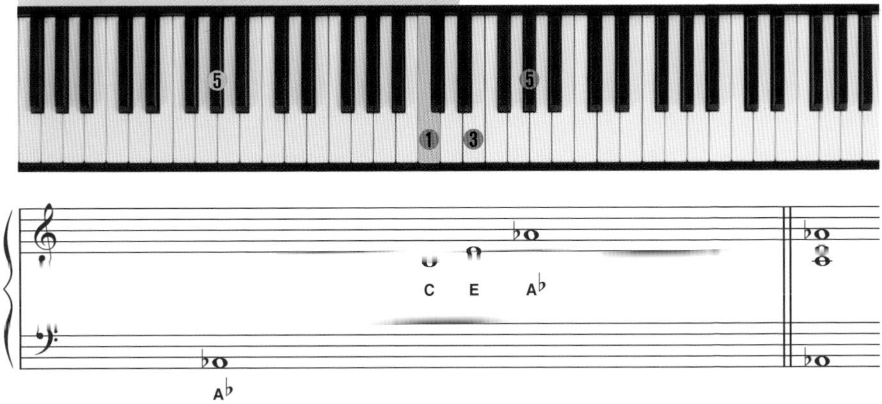

A♭ AUGMENTED TRIAD: 2nd inversion

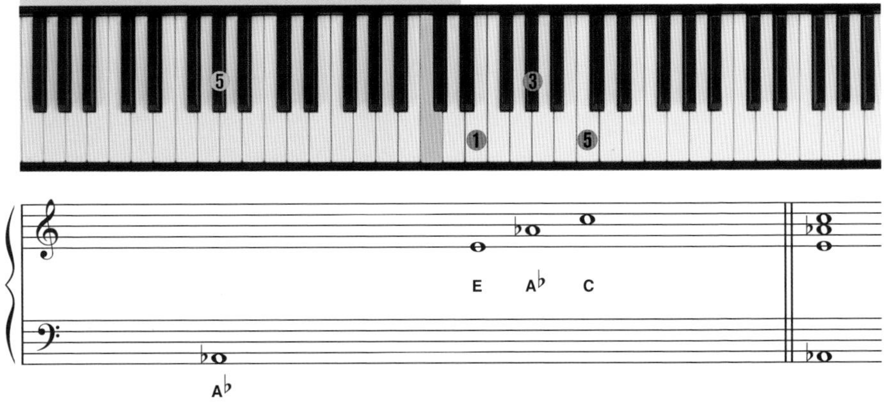

A♭ SUS 4 TRIAD: root position

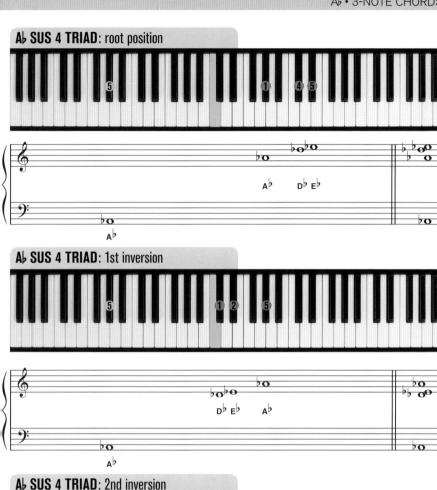

A♭   D♭ E♭

A♭

A♭ SUS 4 TRIAD: 1st inversion

D♭ E♭   A♭

A♭

A♭ SUS 4 TRIAD: 2nd inversion

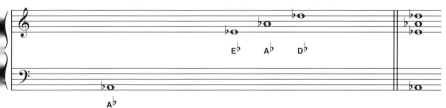

E♭   A♭   D♭

A♭

A♭

A♭ MAJOR 7th: root position

A♭   C   E♭   G

A♭

A♭ MAJOR 7th: 1st inversion

C   E♭   G   A♭

A♭

A♭

A♭ MAJOR 7th: 2nd inversion

E♭   G A♭   C

A♭

A♭ MAJOR 7th: 3rd inversion

G A♭   C   E♭

A♭

A♭

G# MINOR 7th: root position

G# B D# F#

G#

G# MINOR 7th: 1st inversion

A♭

B D# F# G#

G#

G♯ MINOR 7th: 2nd inversion

D♯   F♯ G♯   B

G♯

G♯ MINOR 7th: 3rd inversion

Ab

F♯ G♯   B   D♯

G♯

A♭ DOMINANT 7th: root position

A♭   C   E♭   G♭

A♭

A♭ DOMINANT 7th: 1st inversion

A♭

C   E♭   G♭   A♭

A♭

Ab DOMINANT 7th: 2nd inversion

Eb Gb Ab C

Ab

Ab DOMINANT 7th: 3rd inversion

Gb Ab C Eb

Ab

Ab

G♯ MINOR 7th (♭5): root position

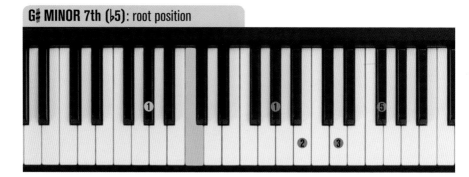

G♯   B   D   F♯

G♯

G♯ MINOR 7th (♭5): 1st inversion

A♭

B   D   F♯   G♯

G♯

G# MINOR 7th (b5): 2nd inversion

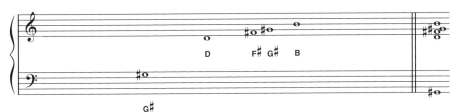

D   F# G#   B

G#

G# MINOR 7th (b5): 3rd inversion

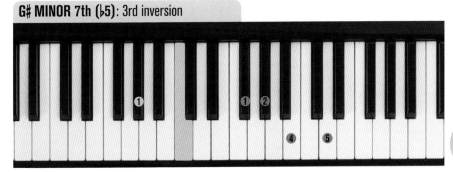

Ab

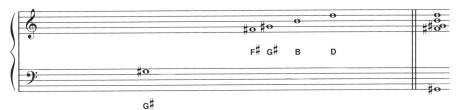

F# G#   B   D

G#

G# DIMINISHED 7th: root position

G#   B   D   F

G#

A♭ MAJOR 7th (#5): root position

A♭

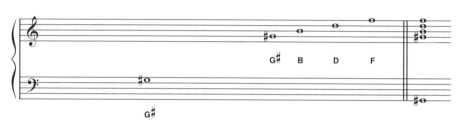

A♭   C   E   G

A♭

Ab MINOR (MAJOR) 7th: root position

Ab   Cb   Eb   G

Ab

Ab MAJOR 7th (#11): root position

Ab   C   D   G

Ab

Ab

A♭ MAJOR 6th: root position

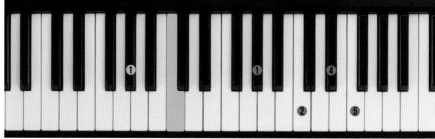

A♭   C   E♭   F

A♭

G♯ MINOR 6th: root position

A♭

G♯   B   D♯   E♯

G♯

A♭ DOMINANT 7th (SUS 4): root position

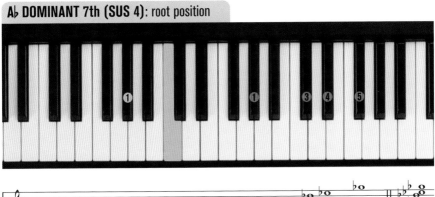

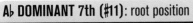

A♭   D♭ E♭   G♭

A♭

A♭ DOMINANT 7th (#11): root position

A♭   C   D   G♭

A♭

A♭

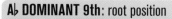

A♭ DOMINANT 9th: root position

C   E♭   G♭   B♭

A♭

G♯ DOMINANT 7th (♭9): root position

A♭

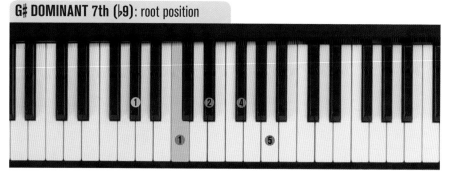

B   D♯   F♯   A

G♯

Ab DOMINANT 13th

Gb   Bb   C   F

Ab

G# DOMINANT 7th (#9, b13)

B#   E   F#   B

G#

Ab

A

If you like "fiddle" music then learn chords in A major and minor, as many jigs and reels are written in these keys. This is so that the violin can use plenty of open string notes in the tune. Other chords to learn if you are accompanying a violin in this style are: G, D, E major, and E minor.

Keying the chords to the composers:

• Beethoven's famous "Für Elise" is in the key of A minor and still remains a firm favorite among beginner piano players of all ages.

• "Lady Madonna" by The Beatles has a great piano part in A major with the piano at the forefront of the arrangement. One strong feature is the use of octaves in the left hand.

• Boogie-woogie piano is a blues-based form that U.K. pianist Jools Holland (b.1958) has done much to popularize. Take, for example, his "Bumble Boogie" in A major, which uses A, D, and E chords in its 12-bar blues sequence.

• "Hurt," the last single by the U.S. country singer-songwriter Johnny Cash (1932–2003), is a piano-based song in A minor, which uses A minor, C, and D major triads in the verse.

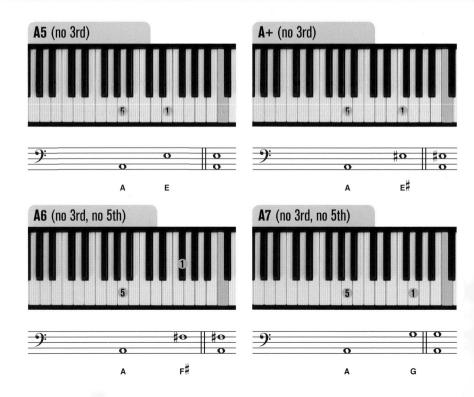

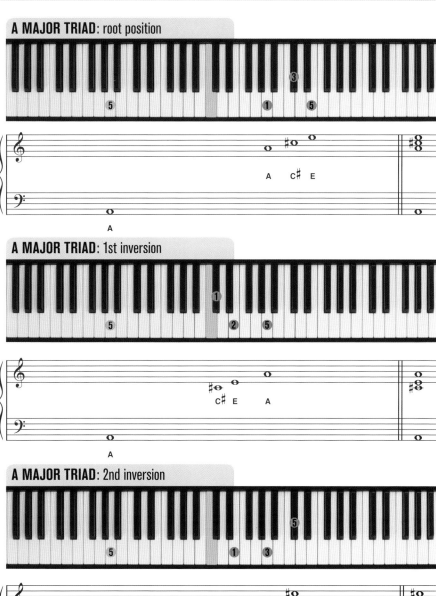

A MAJOR TRIAD: root position

A

A MAJOR TRIAD: 1st inversion

A

A MAJOR TRIAD: 2nd inversion

A

A

A MINOR TRIAD: root position

5   1 3 5

A C E

A

A MINOR TRIAD: 1st inversion

5   1 2 5

C E A

A

A MINOR TRIAD: 2nd inversion

5   1 3 5

E A C

A

A

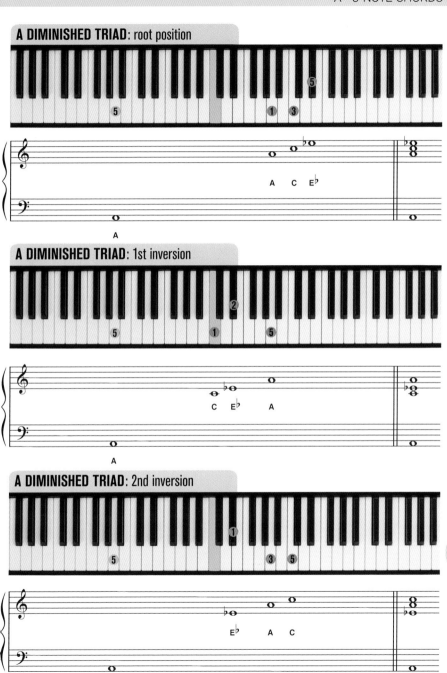

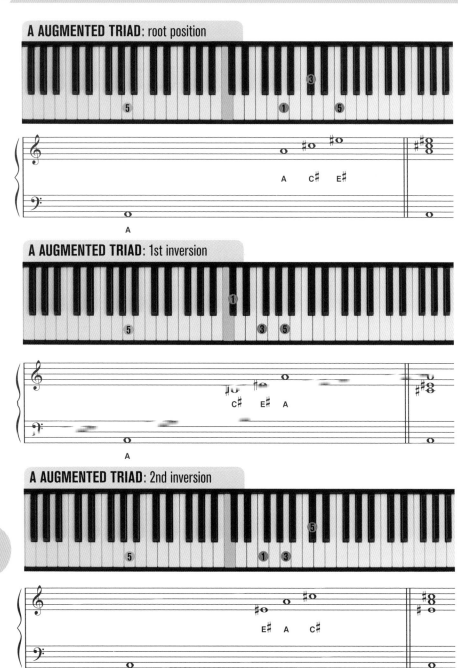

A AUGMENTED TRIAD: root position

A AUGMENTED TRIAD: 1st inversion

A AUGMENTED TRIAD: 2nd inversion

A

A SUS 4 TRIAD: root position

A SUS 4 TRIAD: 1st inversion

A SUS 4 TRIAD: 2nd inversion

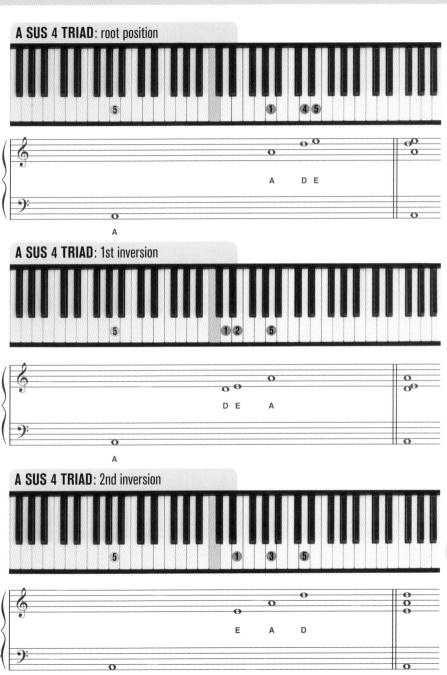

A

A MAJOR 7th: root position

A   C#   E   G#

A

A MAJOR 7th: 1st inversion

A

C#   E   G#A

A

A MAJOR 7th: 2nd inversion

E G#A C#

A

A MAJOR 7th: 3rd inversion

G# A C# E

A

A

A MINOR 7th: root position

A   C   E   G

A

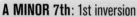

A MINOR 7th: 1st inversion

C   E   G   A

A

A

A MINOR 7th: 2nd inversion

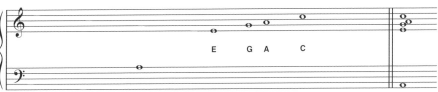

A MINOR 7th: 3rd inversion

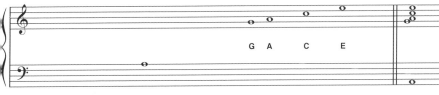

A

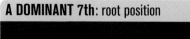

A   C#   E   G

A

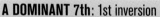

C#   E   G   A

A

A

A DOMINANT 7th: 2nd inversion

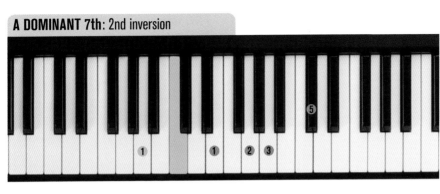

E G A c♯

A

A DOMINANT 7th: 3rd inversion

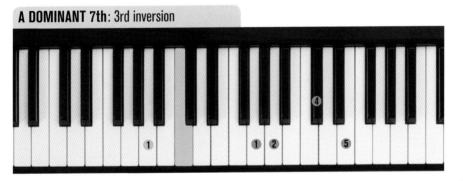

G A c♯ E

A

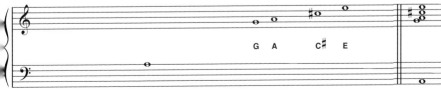

A

A MINOR 7th (♭5): root position

A   C   E♭   G

A

A MINOR 7th (♭5): 1st inversion

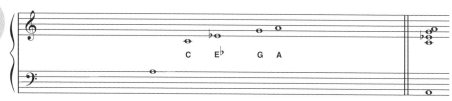

C   E♭   G   A

A

A

A MINOR 7th (♭5): 2nd inversion

E♭ G A C

A

A MINOR 7th (♭5): 3rd inversion

G A C E♭

A

A

A DIMINISHED 7th: root position

A   C   E♭   G♭

A

A MAJOR 7th (#5): root position

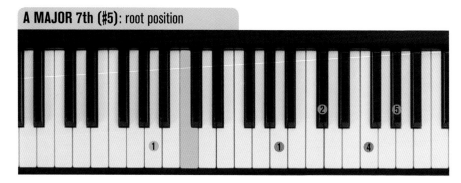

A   C♯   E♯   G♯

A

A

A MINOR (MAJOR) 7th: root position

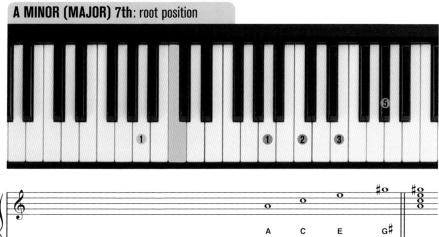

A   C   E   G♯

A

A MAJOR 7th (♯11): root position

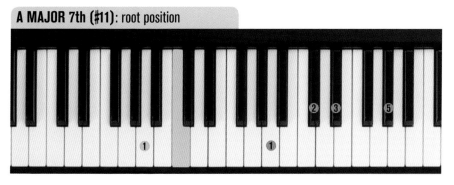

A   C♯ D♯   G♯

A

A MAJOR 6th: root position

A   C#   E   F#

A

A MINOR 6th: root position

A   C   E   F#

A

A

A DOMINANT 7th (SUS 4): root position

A   D   E   G

A

A DOMINANT 7th (#11): root position

A   C#   D#   G

A

A

A DOMINANT 9th: root position

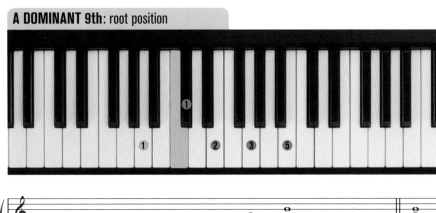

C# E G B

A

A DOMINANT 7th (♭9): root position

C# E G B♭

A

A

A DOMINANT 13th

A G B C♯ F♯

A DOMINANT 7th (♯9, ♭13)

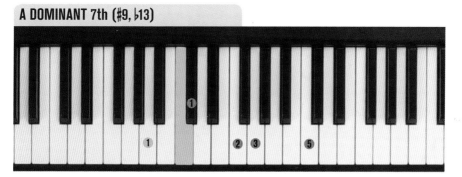

A C♯ F G C

A

B♭/A♯

You'll find that much brass music is written in B♭, so learn the B♭ chords. The trumpet, trombone, and tenor saxophone are all B♭ instruments, and find this key the easiest to play in. As a keyboard player you'll be able to accompany these instruments and play tunes in B♭ with the 3- and 4-note major chords in this chapter, and with E♭ and F chords too.

Keying the chords to the composers:

• Franz Schubert's (1797–1828) Scherzo in B♭ major Op.posth. (Opus Posthumous) for solo piano features B♭ major 2nd inversion triads in the left-hand accompaniment.

• In Queen's famous song "Bohemian Rhapsody" from their 1975 album *A Night At The Opera*, Freddie Mercury's opening solo piano section is in B♭ major. Here he uses a B♭ major 2nd inversion triad, like the one on page 213, with the left hand over playing octaves.

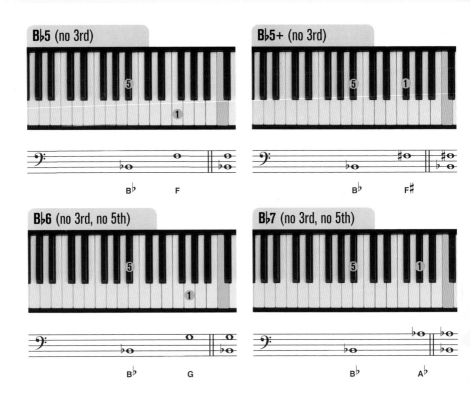

B♭5 (no 3rd)

B♭   F

B♭5+ (no 3rd)

B♭   F♯

B♭6 (no 3rd, no 5th)

B♭   G

B♭7 (no 3rd, no 5th)

B♭   A♭

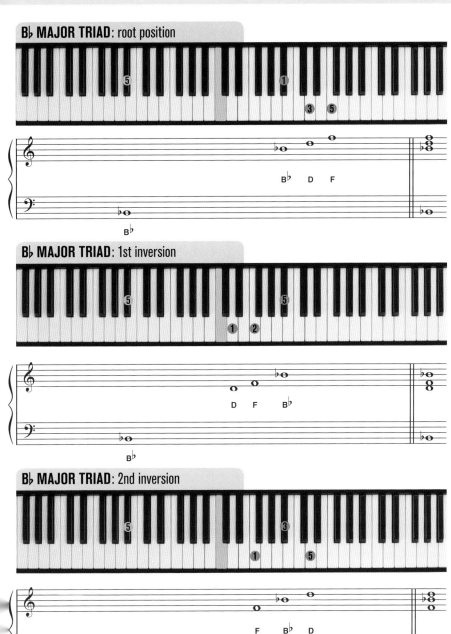

Bb MAJOR TRIAD: root position

Bb D F

Bb

Bb MAJOR TRIAD: 1st inversion

D F Bb

Bb

Bb MAJOR TRIAD: 2nd inversion

F Bb D

Bb

Bb

B♭ MINOR TRIAD: root position

B♭ MINOR TRIAD: 1st inversion

B♭ MINOR TRIAD: 2nd inversion

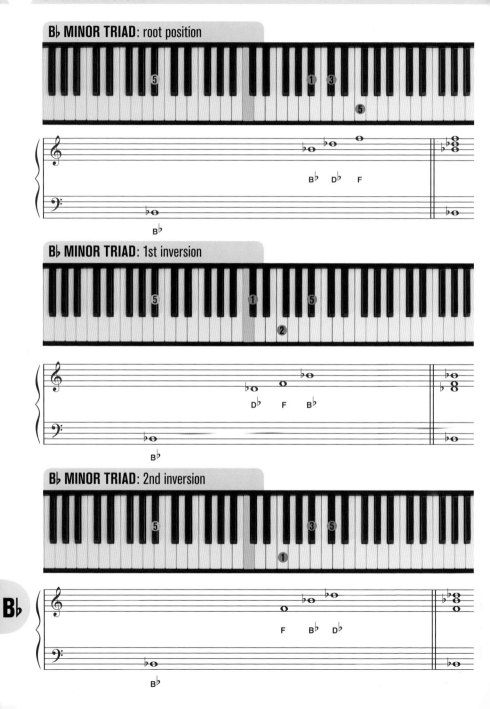

B♭

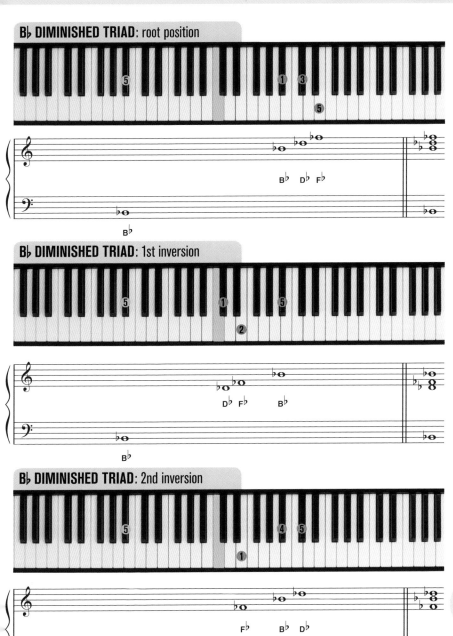

B♭ DIMINISHED TRIAD: root position

B♭ D♭ F♭

B♭

B♭ DIMINISHED TRIAD: 1st inversion

D♭ F♭   B♭

B♭

B♭ DIMINISHED TRIAD: 2nd inversion

F♭   B♭ D♭

B♭

B♭

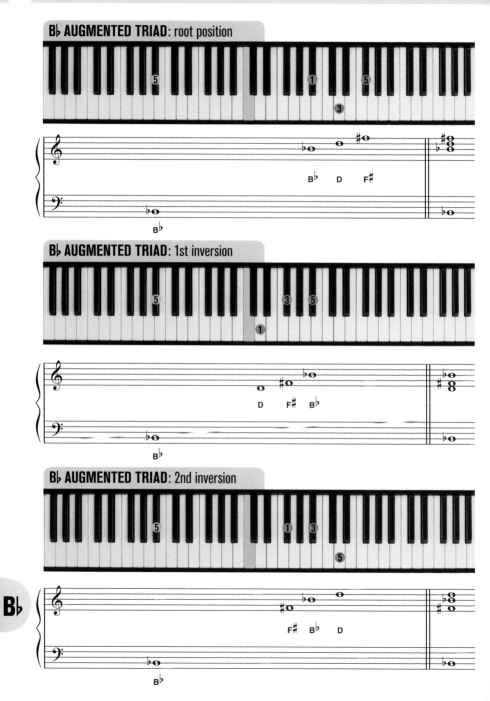

B♭ AUGMENTED TRIAD: root position

B♭ D F♯

B♭

B♭ AUGMENTED TRIAD: 1st inversion

D F♯ B♭

B♭

B♭ AUGMENTED TRIAD: 2nd inversion

F♯ B♭ D

B♭

B♭ SUS 4 TRIAD: root position

B♭ SUS 4 TRIAD: 1st inversion

B♭ SUS 4 TRIAD: 2nd inversion

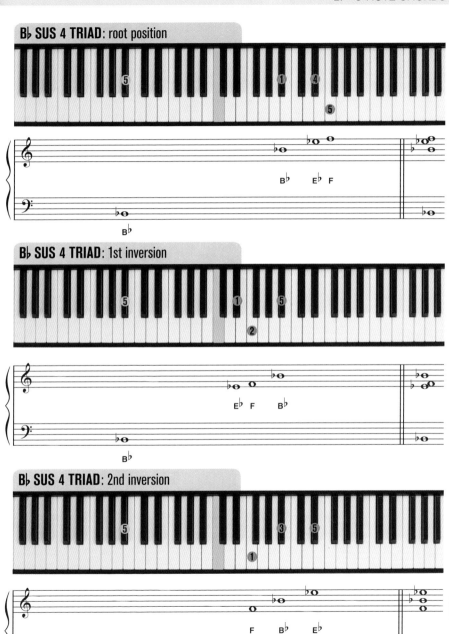

B♭

B♭ MAJOR 7th: root position

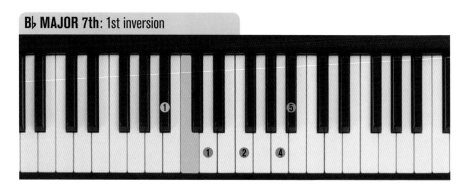

B♭   D   F   A

B♭

B♭ MAJOR 7th: 1st inversion

D   F   A B♭

B♭

B♭

B♭ MAJOR 7th: 2nd inversion

F   A B♭   D

B♭

B♭ MAJOR 7th: 3rd inversion

A B♭   D   F

B♭

B♭

B♭ MINOR 7th: root position

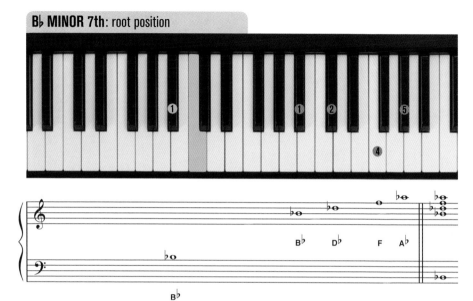

B♭ MINOR 7th: 1st inversion

B♭

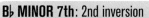

Bb MINOR 7th: 2nd inversion

F   Ab Bb   Db

Bb

Bb MINOR 7th: 3rd inversion

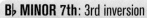

Ab Bb   Db   F

Bb

Bb

B♭ DOMINANT 7th: root position

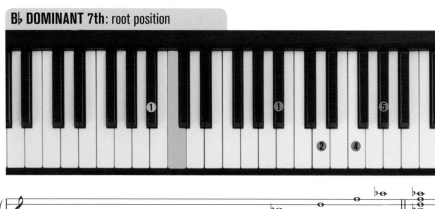

B♭ DOMINANT 7th: 1st inversion

B♭

Bb DOMINANT 7th: 2nd inversion

F   Ab   Bb   D

Bb

Bb DOMINANT 7th: 3rd inversion

Ab   Bb   D   F

Bb

Bb

A# MINOR 7th (♭5): root position

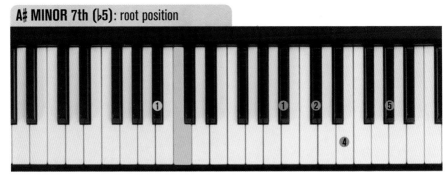

A#   C#   E   G#

A#

A# MINOR 7th (♭5): 1st inversion

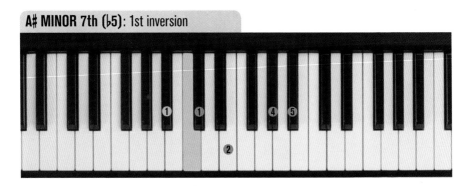

C#   E   G# A#

A#

B♭

A♯ MINOR 7th (♭5): 2nd inversion

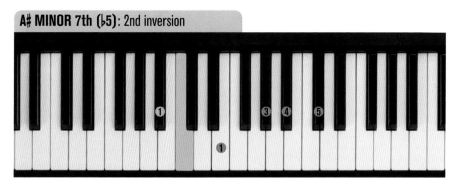

E   G♯ A♯   C♯

A♯

A♯ MINOR 7th (♭5): 3rd inversion

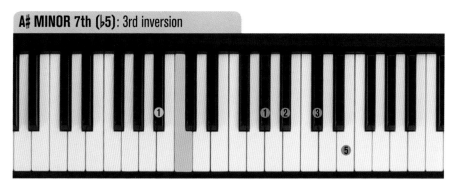

G♯ A♯   C♯   E

A♯

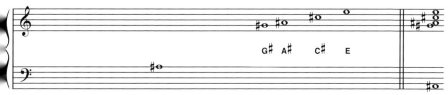

B♭

A# DIMINISHED 7th: root position

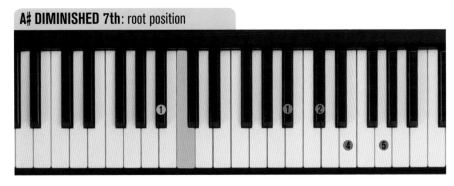

A# C# E G

A#

Bb MAJOR 7th (#5): root position

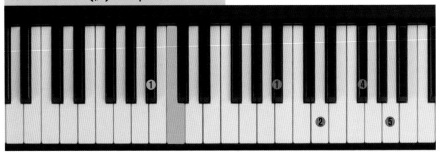

Bb D F# A

Bb

Bb

B♭ MINOR (MAJOR) 7th: root position

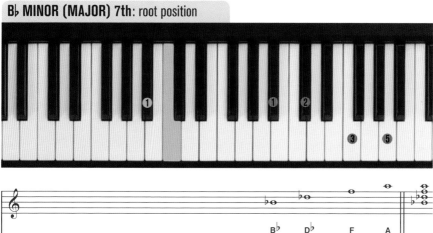

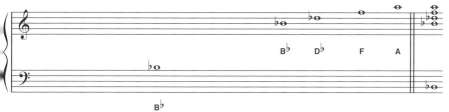

B♭   D♭   F   A

B♭

B♭ MAJOR 7th (♯11): root position

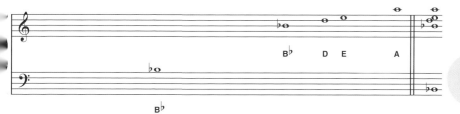

B♭   D   E   A

B♭

B♭

B♭ MAJOR 6th: root position

B♭   D   F   G

B♭

B♭ MINOR 6th: root position

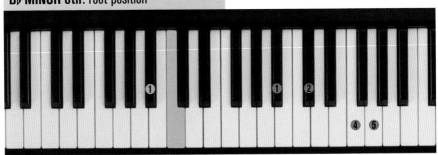

B♭   D♭   F   G

B♭

B♭

Bb DOMINANT 7th (SUS 4): root position

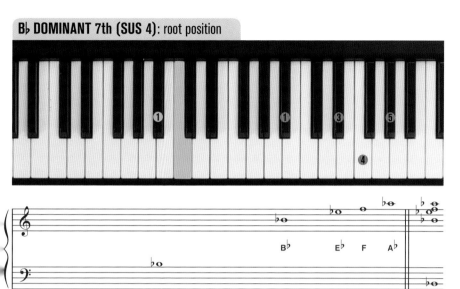

Bb   Eb   F   Ab

Bb

Bb DOMINANT 7th (#11): root position

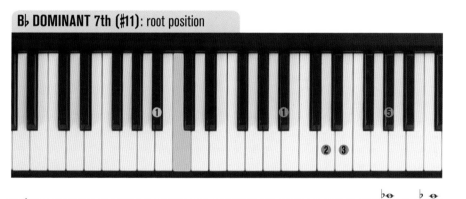

Bb   D   E   Ab

Bb

Bb

B♭ DOMINANT 9th: root position

D   F   A♭   C

B♭

B♭ DOMINANT 7th (♭9): root position

D   F   A♭   C♭

B♭

B♭

Bb DOMINANT 13th

Bb   Ab   C   D   G

Bb DOMINANT 7th (#9, b13)

Bb   D   Gb Ab   Db

Bb

B

Chords have distinct sounds and feelings, and the more you work with them, the more you will discover this for yourself. Listen hard to the arrangement of notes for each chord and you'll gradually find ones that you are drawn to. Beethoven and many other composers have described keys and chords as being bright or dark and have even associated them with particular colors.

Keying the chords to the composers:

• Frédéric Chopin's Prelude in B minor Op.28, No.6 is a beautiful example of triad use in both hands—the left hand melody is built from a root

position B minor triad, and the first chord of the right hand is a B minor triad in 1st inversion (page 234).

• "You Are The Sunshine Of My Life" by Stevie Wonder, from the wonderful *Talking Book* album of 1972, opens in B major with its distinctive use of an F♯ augmented triad and whole-tone scale in the introduction.

• In 2006, the English band Anathema recorded a song "One Last Goodbye" on their album *Judgement*, featuring piano in B minor with much use of G and A major triads.

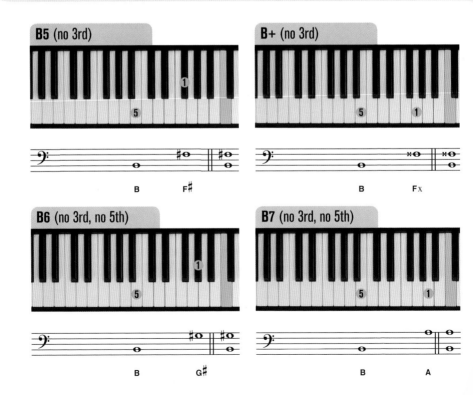

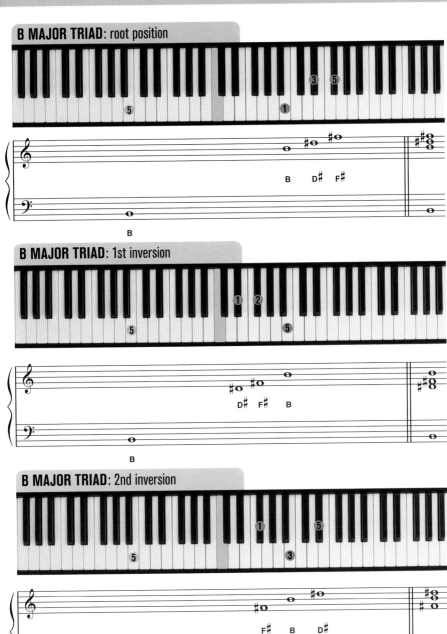

B MAJOR TRIAD: root position

B   D♯   F♯

B

B MAJOR TRIAD: 1st inversion

D♯   F♯   B

B

B MAJOR TRIAD: 2nd inversion

F♯   B   D♯

B

B

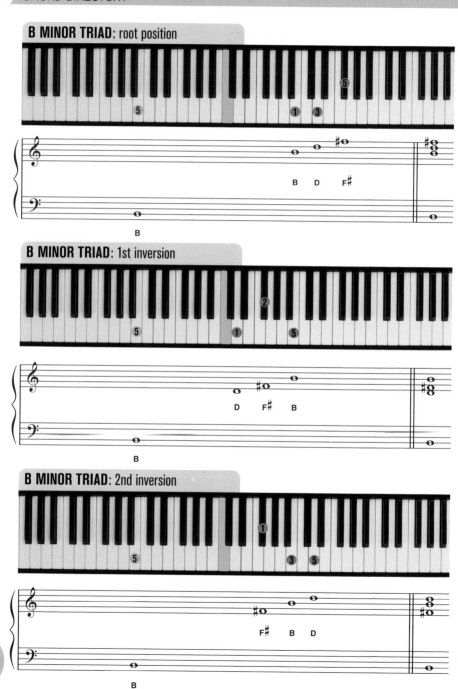

B MINOR TRIAD: root position

B D F#

B

B MINOR TRIAD: 1st inversion

D F# B

B

B MINOR TRIAD: 2nd inversion

F# B D

B

B

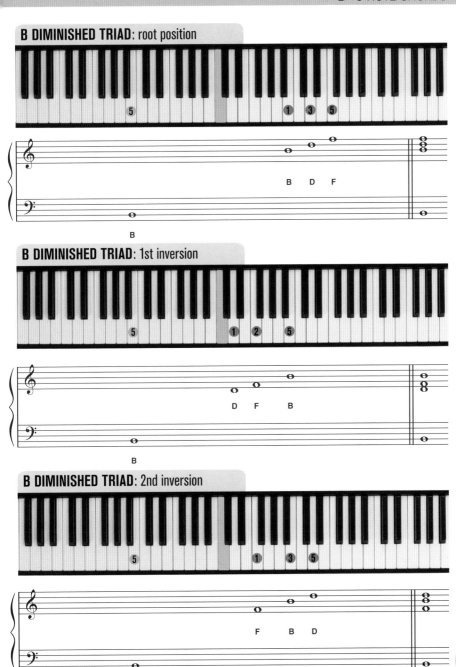

B DIMINISHED TRIAD: root position

B   D   F

B

B DIMINISHED TRIAD: 1st inversion

D   F   B

B

B DIMINISHED TRIAD: 2nd inversion

F   B   D

B

B

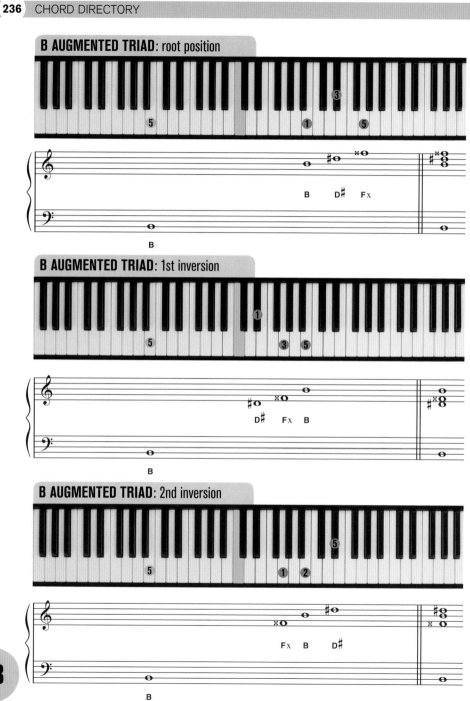

B AUGMENTED TRIAD: root position

B   D♯   F✕

B

B AUGMENTED TRIAD: 1st inversion

D♯   F✕   B

B

B AUGMENTED TRIAD: 2nd inversion

F✕   B   D♯

B

B

B SUS 4 TRIAD: root position

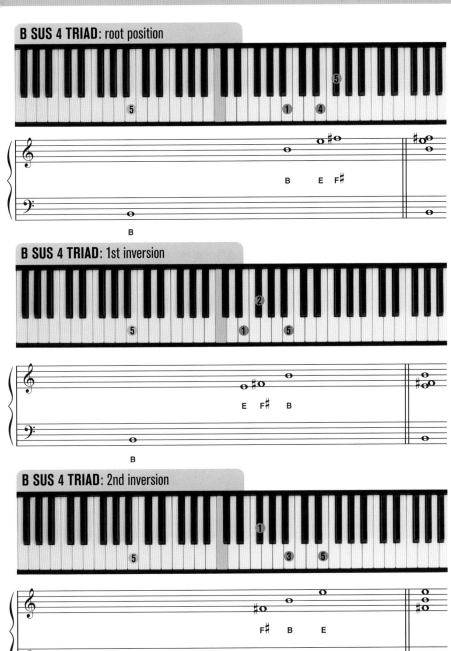

B   E   F#

B

B SUS 4 TRIAD: 1st inversion

E   F#   B

B

B SUS 4 TRIAD: 2nd inversion

F#   B   E

B

B

B MAJOR 7th: root position

B MAJOR 7th: 1st inversion

B

B MAJOR 7th: 2nd inversion

F♯   A♯ B   D♯

B

B MAJOR 7th: 3rd inversion

A♯ B   D♯   F♯

B

B MINOR 7th: root position

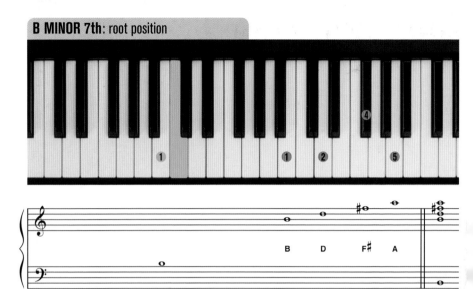

B D F♯ A

B

B MINOR 7th: 1st inversion

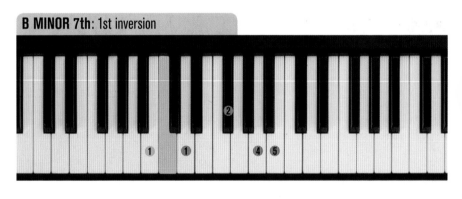

D F♯ A B

B

B

B MINOR 7th: 2nd inversion

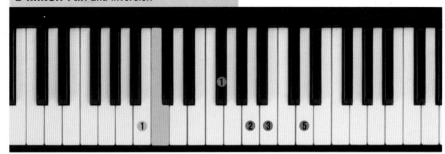

F# A B D

B

B MINOR 7th: 3rd inversion

A B D F#

B

B

B DOMINANT 7th: root position

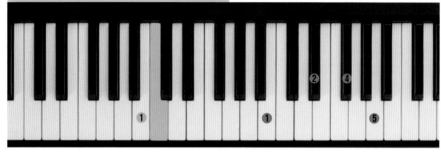

B   D♯   F♯   A

B

B DOMINANT 7th: 1st inversion

D♯   F♯   A   B

B

B

B DOMINANT 7th: 2nd inversion

F#   A   B   D#

B

B DOMINANT 7th: 3rd inversion

A   B   D#   F#

B

B

B MINOR 7th (♭5): root position

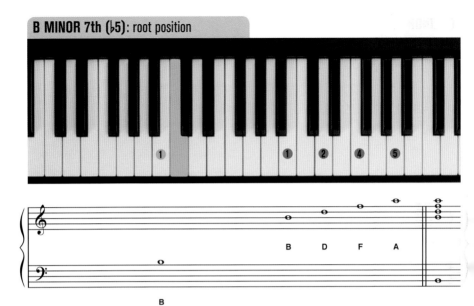

B   D   F   A

B

B MINOR 7th (♭5): 1st inversion

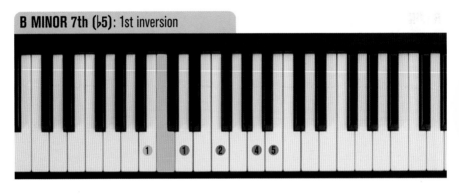

D   F   A B

B

B

B MINOR 7th (♭5): 2nd inversion

F   A   B   D

B

B MINOR 7th (♭5): 3rd inversion

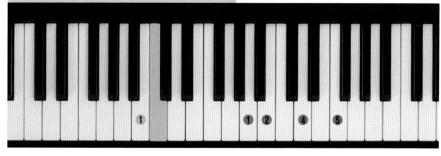

A   B   D   F

B

B

B DIMINISHED 7th: root position

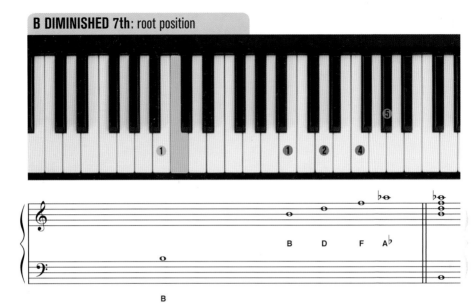

B D F A♭

B

B MAJOR 7th (#5): root position

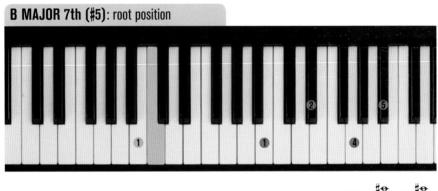

B D♯ Fx A♯

B

B

B MINOR (MAJOR) 7th: root position

B   D   F♯   A♯

B

B MAJOR 7th (♯11): root position

B   D♯   E♯   A♯

B

B

B MAJOR 6th: root position

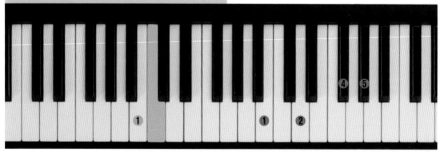

B   D♯   F♯   G♯

B

B MINOR 6th: root position

B   D   F♯   G♯

B

B

B DOMINANT 7th (SUS 4): root position

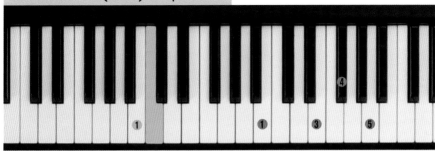

B E F♯ A

B

B DOMINANT 7th (♯11): root position

B D♯ E♯ A

B

B

B DOMINANT 9th: root position

D♯   F♯   A   C♯

B

B DOMINANT 7th (♭9): root position

D♯   F♯   A   C

B

B

B DOMINANT 13th

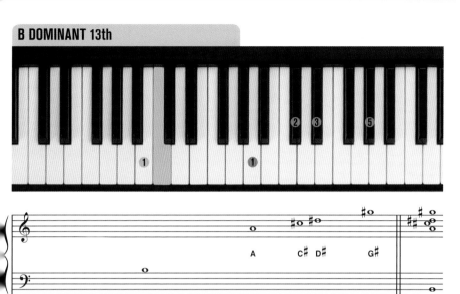

B   A   C♯   D♯   G♯

B DOMINANT 7th (♯9, ♭13)

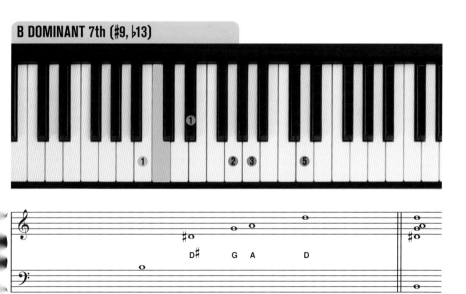

B   D♯   G   A   D

B

Glossary

Accidental
Sign that modifies the pitch of the note when placed before it. A sharp (♯) raises a note one semitone; a flat (♭) lowers a note one semitone.

Augmented
When the 5th note of a triad is raised or sharpened it is called an augmented chord.

Bass clef
Usually indicates the music to be played by the left hand. The bass clef is also called the F clef and the clef fixes the note F on the 4th line of the stave.

Bass note
This is the bottom note of a chord, usually found in the left hand. Nearly all the bass notes in this book are doubling the bottom note of the chord at least an octave below.

Broken chord
Play the notes of a chord separately, from the bottom note upward or the top note downward, and this is a broken chord. Many accompaniment patterns are based on broken chord shapes.

Chord sequence
One chord played after another different chord to create a tune or song.

Diminished
When the 5th note of a chord is lowered or flattened it is diminished. A pure diminished chord has three semitone steps between each note, from the bottom upwards.

Dominant 7th
Dominant is the musical name for the 5th note of the major or minor scale. The dominant 7th chord is the 4-note chord built on that note stacked in thirds. There is a tension in the dominant 7th chord that is best resolved by the chord built on the first note of the scale (tonic), and the resulting sequence is one of the most important chord sounds in Western music.

Doubling
When you add a note to a chord that is an octave higher or lower than one of the notes already in the chord, you are "doubling" that note.

Enharmonic
Notes that share the same sound, but have different names (e.g. C♯ or D♭).

Flat (♭)
Symbol used to lower the note by one semitone.

Harmonic minor scale
A set of notes used to build chords in Western music. Directly related to the major scale, these chords create rich harmonies.

Inversion
A chord is inverted if a note other than the root is its bass note.

Key signature
Group of sharps or flats placed to the right of the clef on a stave to identify the key.

Major chord
Most consonant (or stable) chord in music. A triad is constructed from the 1st, 3rd, and 5th degrees of the major scale. Often described as a "happy"-sounding chord.

Major scale
This is the most important scale in Western music. Stack the notes of this scale up in thirds and you will build most of the chords in this book.

Melodic minor scale
This scale is used to create smooth minor melodies, but it is still related directly to the major scale. Good harmonies can be built with this scale but it is best used to create minor tunes.

Minor chord
Slightly less consonant than a major chord, and constructed from the 1st, 3rd, and 5th degrees of the harmonic minor scale. Often described as a "sad"-sounding chord.

Natural (♮)
Neither sharp nor flat, a natural cancels out the accidental to restore the note to its original pitch.

Natural minor scale
An important scale used in Western music to create melodies and build chords.

Octave
Interval formed by two notes of which the upper has twice the frequency of the lower. They have the same note name and are found eight notes apart on the keyboard.

Credits

Quarto would like to thanks and acknowledge the following for supplying illustrations and photographs reproduced in this book:

iStockphoto images
Shutterstock Photos

All other illustrations and photographs are the copyright of Quarto Publishing plc. While every effort has been made to credit contributors, Quarto would like to apologize should there have been any omissions or errors—and would be pleased to make the appropriate correction for future editions of the book.

Acknowledgements

Gillian Gardiner for your love and support. Dave Hewson for continued inspiration. Kate, Anna and Chlöe at Quarto for putting it all together.

...and Dad—look at me now!